"God is raising up a great compan̦ impact every sphere of society in order to gloriously advance His Kingdom. *Fueled by Fire* by Staci Wallace will inspire, empower and equip those whose hearts passionately desire to serve the Lord in this strategic hour."

Patricia King, founder, Women in Ministry Network

"*Wow!* What a timely word for such a time as this! Staci has once again hit it out of the park with *Fueled by Fire*. There is no question that God speaks through Staci in a bold, prophetic and timely manner. I come from a background of domestic violence, molestation, incarceration and homelessness, among many other things. Staci took me into her home, showed me that I have value and I have a future. There are so many other women who feel alone, lost, abandoned and unworthy. I pray that this book reaches every one of them. You are beautiful, powerful and so treasured. Staci is the most anointed person I know, and she has a boldness and audacity that God uses to pierce the darkness and bring light everywhere she goes. I am so honored and proud to call Staci Wallace my mentor, leader, teacher and, most of all, friend. It is a privilege to work side by side reaching the lost and broken. I love you, dear friend, and I could not be more proud of you! May *Fueled by Fire* reach the hands of every woman and girl who needs to find her identity and worth in you, Father God."

Christina Willis, CRMA; director of outreach, EMwomen

"I met Staci Wallace back in the early 1980s. We spent our teenage years together seeking affirmation and purpose. It is no wonder that she has dedicated her life to empowering women. Through the years I have witnessed the impact she has had on countless lives. *Fueled by Fire* is a power-packed tool to unleash the unique purpose within."

Jill Chambers, author, speaker, behavioral consultant

"*Fueled by Fire* is a *now* word for women. The Lord is moving and stirring the hearts of His daughters to get clear direction, encouragement, deep connection and a battle plan to initiate the next season of *awakening* in the Body of Christ. This book will challenge and motivate you to step into your fullest calling as a daughter of the Most High God! Thank you, Staci, for bringing that battle cry to life!"

Chef Tiffany Poe, CEC; Write Your Life Recipe Ministries

"It's time to realize the power you really have inside you! This book wakes your spirit up with awareness it has never experienced before. It gives you strength and strategies to face reality with confidence, opens your eyes and brings freedom! It is a revelation to victory that will change your life. Take it and run!"

Sandra Gosser, MSN, NNP-BC

"*Fueled By Fire* is a powerful work that will you show you how to achieve success through the Holy Spirit working supernaturally in your life to achieve things you never thought possible."

Terry D. Toler, author, *How to Make More Than a Million Dollars, The Jesus Diet* and *The Eden Stories*

"God said to me, *Read Staci's manuscript!* I cannot tell you the last time I read a full book practically nonstop . . . much less read anything other than a text, DM or email! The enemy knew the words that were written by Staci! He knew the words that I would read! He knew the words would empower *me* to become a godly woman, the queen of *my* kingdom, wearing *my* crown, *my* breastplate and holding *my* sword! Thank you, Staci, my sister in God, for this blessing of reading your *EMpowering* words!"

Cynthia Griner, chief creative officer, Ludlow BAS

FUELED
by
FIRE

FUELED *by* FIRE

BECOMING A WOMAN OF

Courage, Faith and Influence

STACI WALLACE

Chosen

a division of Baker Publishing Group
Minneapolis, Minnesota

Published by Chosen Books
11400 Hampshire Avenue South
Bloomington, Minnesota 55438
www.chosenbooks.com

Chosen Books is a division of
Baker Publishing Group, Grand Rapids, Michigan

Printed in the United States of America

ISBN 978-0-8007-6179-0 (paperback)
ISBN 978-0-8007-6218-6 (casebound)

Library of Congress Control Number: 2020943484

Unless otherwise indicated, Scripture quotations are from THE HOLY BIBLE, NEW INTERNATIONAL VERSION®, NIV® Copyright © 1973, 1978, 1984, 2011 by Biblica, Inc.® Used by permission. All rights reserved worldwide.

Scripture quotations labeled AMPC are from the Amplified® Bible (AMPC), copyright © 1954, 1958, 1962, 1964, 1965, 1987 by The Lockman Foundation. Used by permission. www.Lockman.org

Scripture quotations labeled BSB are from The Holy Bible, Berean Study Bible, BSB, copyright © 2016, 2018, 2019 by Bible Hub. Used by permission. All rights reserved worldwide.

Scripture quotations labeled ESV are from The Holy Bible, English Standard Version® (ESV®), copyright © 2001 by Crossway, a publishing ministry of Good News Publishers. Used by permission. All rights reserved. ESV Text Edition: 2016

Scripture quotations labeled HCSB are from the Holman Christian Standard Bible®, copyright © 1999, 2000, 2002, 2003, 2009 by Holman Bible Publishers. Used by permission. Holman Christian Standard Bible®, Holman CSB®, and HCSB® are federally registered trademarks of Holman Bible Publishers.

Scripture quotations labeled KJV are from the King James Version of the Bible.

Scripture quotations labeled MSG are taken from THE MESSAGE, copyright © 1993, 2002, 2018 by Eugene H. Peterson. Used by permission of NavPress. All rights reserved. Represented by Tyndale House Publishers, Inc.

Scripture quotations labeled NASB are from the New American Standard Bible® (NASB), copyright © 1960, 1962, 1963, 1968, 1971, 1972, 1973, 1975, 1977, 1995 by The Lockman Foundation. Used by permission. www.Lockman.org

Scripture quotations labeled NKJV are from the New King James Version®. Copyright © 1982 by Thomas Nelson. Used by permission. All rights reserved.

Scripture quotations labeled NLT are taken from the Holy Bible, New Living Translation, copyright © 1996, 2004, 2015 by Tyndale House Foundation. Used by permission of Tyndale House Publishers, Inc., Carol Stream, Illinois 60188. All rights reserved.

Scripture quotations labeled TLB are from The Living Bible, copyright © 1971. Used by permission of Tyndale House Publishers, Inc., Carol Stream, Illinois 60188. All rights reserved.

In some cases, the names of individuals and identifying details have been changed to protect privacy.

Cover design by Rob Williams, InsideOutCreativeArts

The author is represented by Literary Management Group

In keeping with biblical principles of creation stewardship, Baker Publishing Group advocates the responsible use of our natural resources. As a member of the Green Press Initiative, our company uses recycled paper when possible. The text paper of this book is composed in part of post-consumer waste.

20 21 22 23 24 25 26   7 6 5 4 3 2 1

This book is for the woman who wonders if her life truly has significance. She has worked hard to keep her ship sailing but wonders if she will ever get to the other side of her journey and whether or not she will leave an impact on this world as she had hoped. She longs for peace and works for profits, but deep inside her heart, she knows she was born for something greater.

Unimpressed with the popular rhetoric about female liberation, she is fully persuaded that God has uniquely ordained her womanhood for greatness and is determined to see it radiate His brilliance. She is unmoved by the common message that tries to get her to compete with the men or masculine energy around her. She is, instead, moved to find the sweet spot of collaboration that allows God to use her beautiful femininity to partner with God's greater humanity.

Now is the time for a new generation of confident women of God to arise and be empowered by the Holy Spirit to launch into greater places of influence. You are that woman. You are about to turn your success into significance and your mess into a message of hope for millions. You are powerful beyond words, and when you are fueled by fire, *nothing will be impossible*.

This book is *for you*!

Contents

Foreword

When I met Staci Wallace in September 2018, my husband and I had just jumped into the most radical *yes* that we had ever given Jesus. In our 25–plus years of marriage and full-time ministry, we have walked out a life of obedience to the Lord and given Him our surrender over and over again. But in 2017, for the second time in our lives, He asked us to walk away from a secure, prestigious position as worship pastors at a megachurch and launch out into the unknown once again.

I have found that God typically does not hand out the details of where He is leading us when He invites us to follow. He is simply looking for a trusting heart with a *yes* that does not pick and choose but offers complete obedience, knowing that is where the abundant life is found that Jesus talked about in John 10.

My heart connected with Staci's immediately, and I soon discovered that she and her husband were also in the middle of walking out their radical *yes* to Jesus. It is no wonder we connected. Deep calls to deep. They, too, had stepped into the unknown, following Jesus with complete surrender.

This type of surrender precedes the fueled-by-fire life. In whatever sphere of influence you operate, God is looking for your complete surrender to Him so that He can use you for Kingdom purposes. Humanity is God's *magnum opus*, His greatest work. When it came to creating humanity, God did not speak us into existence as He did all other creation, but He formed and shaped us into His image. It is the greatest privilege to partner with God to reach His magnum opus through the platform and influence He has given uniquely to each one of us.

Before He ascended into heaven, Jesus left us with the Great Commission. I like how the Message translation states this Commission:

> "Go out and train everyone you meet, far and near, in this way of life, marking them by baptism in the threefold name: Father, Son, and Holy Spirit. Then instruct them in the practice of all I have commanded you."
>
> Matthew 28:19–20 MSG

Days after Jesus issued this Great Commission, the outpouring of the Holy Spirit came into the Upper Room, where the devoted were waiting on the Lord for this great promise. Scripture describes this outpouring of the Spirit as "tongues of fire that separated and came to rest on each of them" (Acts 2:3). A crowd of God-fearing Jews from every nation under heaven heard the sound coming from the Upper Room and began to gather. They said, "We hear them declaring the wonders of God in our own tongues!" (Acts 2:11). When filled with the fire of the Holy Spirit, believers were able to speak in a language that penetrated the hearts of those who had not yet received the revelation of Jesus, and many were saved!

There is no doubt that the marketplace is the sphere of influence God has given Staci Wallace. Because of her success in business and her complete surrender to Jesus to lay it all down and follow Him wherever He says to go, she functions in an authority in this system that is powerful and unique. And she is anointed to impart this authority to you. But until you give Jesus *your* radical *yes*, her words will be only information. With your complete surrender to

Jesus, Staci's words in this book will bring transformation into your life.

The following Scripture has become a life verse for me as I continue to walk out my *yes*, and I believe it is key in living a life fueled by fire:

> Whatever God has promised gets stamped with the Yes of Jesus. In him, this is what we preach and pray, the great Amen, God's Yes and our Yes together, gloriously evident. God affirms us, making us a sure thing in Christ, putting his Yes within us. By his Spirit he has stamped us with his eternal pledge—a sure beginning of what he is destined to complete.
>
> 2 Corinthians 1:20–22 MSG

Nicole Binion, worship recording artist;
co-pastor, Dwell Church

Preface

What happens when a woman walks in the power of the Spirit?

She begins to defy her broken emotions, elevates beyond logic, silences her critics, rises up over fear and doubt, leads armies and breaks records. Her pursuit is not the applause of others, nor is she motivated by rhetoric calling her to appease a feminist agenda. But she hungers to use her femininity to reflect the nurturing and reproductive heart of God to her generation.

A woman who is empowered by the Holy Spirit and fueled by His fire knows she has been set apart with a higher purpose to set captives free, break chains of bondage, negotiate on behalf of legacy, birth revolutions and save generations by her willingness to risk failure and become a force of change in the world.

So let me ask you, "What fuels you?" What causes you to wake up every morning and step out of your comfort zone with a purpose and a passion to break records? For Olympic athletes, that fuel may be the dream of a gold medal. For a new mom, it may be the precious sounds of her newborn baby. For entrepreneurs, it may be the passion to do more, acquire more or achieve more.

- What makes you want to get up every morning and determine to never give up?
- What makes you refuse to hit snooze on the alarm clock because it drives you to use the day to move one step closer to your dream?
- What will drive you beyond success and give you the fuel you need to leave an imprint on this world? Is it your family? Is it your job? Is it your spouse? Or could it be something more . . . perhaps something that has been missing in your life?

That is what this book is about—helping you find a fire on the inside so you can become the superhero you were born to be.

Girl, there is a reason you are reading this book. You *know* God has more for you than what you are currently getting, and your hunger drives you to find out how to get the most out of life. No matter what your history looks like or what you had to do to make it here, God is about to use your history to leave a legacy of hope, help and healing for the world around you.

Fueled by Fire is a "how-to" book written to equip you with the spiritual mindset and toolset you need to have supernatural discernment in the boardroom, wisdom in the classroom, compassion at home and the miracle-working power of God in every area of your life. You will receive clear instructions on how to cooperate with your God-given destiny as His conduit of miracles, abundance, spiritual authority and financial prosperity to the people around you.

This book is not meant to make you comfortable. On the contrary, it was written to disrupt the status quo, awaken your spirit and ignite your passion for taking action so that, together, we can make change happen in this world. Now is the time for you to break out of mediocrity and start winning again. You may not realize it, but God has been intricately preparing you for years "for such a time as this" (Esther 4:14).

Introduction

B.O.O.M. (Breaking Out of Mediocrity)

Several years ago, I had been hearing social buzz about the premiere of the new *Wonder Woman* movie. I am not usually an avid movie fan, and I often tend to be one of those people who overspiritualize movies, especially if they do not give credit to God as the supreme source of "all power." But for some reason, when I heard they were bringing *Wonder Woman* back to the big screen, I was filled with anticipation. Maybe it was because people had called me Wonder Woman and Warrior Queen for years. Perhaps it was watching popular culture and recognizing a spiritual shift in the marketplace all around me. Great attention was suddenly being put on female leadership, the Me-too movement, hyperfeminism and now a sudden resurgence of superheroines in popular culture.

We bought our tickets the moment they went on sale, and to commemorate my excitement, my sweet family bought me a Wonder Woman T-shirt, coffee mug and set of gold-trimmed Wonder Woman dinnerware. Clearly, they were equally as excited to see what this new Princess Warrior film would offer. After opening the many presents, I fell asleep that night with great excitement in my heart.

The next morning, at three o'clock, I woke up with the word *supersonic* resonating in my mind. I rolled over and tried to fall back to sleep, but the word continued to flash in my consciousness like neon lights on Broadway. Dragging myself out of bed that morning was not easy, but I knew I needed to look up and meditate on the word *supersonic*. What did it mean? What was the Holy Spirit trying to say to me? So I wiped my eyes, rolled out of bed and shuffled to my office.

Dreams have always been one of the primary ways God has spoken to me during some of my most trying times of sorrow and during some of my biggest business negotiations. Dreams have given me courage and wisdom to know how to take dominion in boardrooms, pray for the sick, execute strategies in business that required great boldness and even find direction on how to raise my children during the chaos of puberty. When a dream with such a clear message makes its way into my subconscious, I take heed to what is being said.

This dream came during a season of great transition in our lives. Just over a year earlier, the company I worked with closed its doors suddenly and unexpectedly. I was a senior vice president and had to shift companies practically overnight. Thankfully, God directed me into another season of financial success, but for some reason, I was feeling unfulfilled and unsettled in my spirit. According to the world's standards, I was winning, but oftentimes a lingering emptiness deep inside left me curled up in the fetal position, crying out for understanding.

What was happening to me? Why all the up-and-down emotions despite the success? My husband, Larry, looked at me one day and jokingly said, "Are you okay? Honey, why are you so sad? Could you be going through menopause?" Risky statement for a man to make, but we both knew something was off. He is lucky I was as baffled as he was because them there are fighting words where I am from! We laughed about it because my emotions were all over the map and I had no explanation why. Then it dawned on me: I very well could be going through the Big M. Maybe that explained why I was feeling so disturbed despite the blessings all around.

After thirty years in business and ministry, I have learned that life is like a roller coaster. The highs and lows are not by accident. Great roller coaster architects design the ups and downs to create intentional moments of shift that equate to a thrilling ride that makes you say, "Let's do it again!" Similarly, the roller coaster of life God has allowed us to experience is not designed to scare us but to shift us from one season to the next. God uses the highs to inspire us and the lows to empower us to dig deeper, grow stronger and gain greater wisdom for what lies ahead. Sometimes pain births new beginnings, and setbacks are actually a set*up* for something beautiful on the horizon.

My first thought that morning after waking up to the word *supersonic* was that maybe God was telling us to start a Sonic Drive-In franchise. I love Sonic's Cherry Limeades, and several friends have had great success with the franchise. But surely God did not wake me up to give me a vision about selling cheeseburgers and tater tots. As I suspected, after studying *supersonic* it became abundantly clear that I was downloading a message from heaven that was greater than the thought of starting a fast-food restaurant and much more eternally significant.

I discovered that the word *supersonic* means a speed greater than sound. A sonic boom is the sound associated with shock waves created when an object travels through the air faster than the speed of sound, creating a boom or explosion to the human ear. Not only does this supersonic boom occur at anywhere from Mach 1 to Mach 5, but there is also such thing as a Mach 5 to 10 hypersonic boom. Then there is a Mach 10 to 25 superhypersonic boom, which is even more powerful. Lastly, what happens beyond

Mach 25 is called a reentry boom, which is so powerful it can trigger earthquakes and shake the planet.[1]

Maybe you are wondering where I am going with this story and what it has to do with seeing the movie *Wonder Woman*. Snap on your seat belt, because I am about to show you something that literally changed my life and my perspective on power.

First, please know that I am by no means qualified to talk about scientific discoveries. Quite frankly, I dropped out of college to start my own business, and science was not my favorite subject in school because I was focused primarily on three things: basketball, music and theatre. Perhaps that was to my advantage because today I cannot attribute my success in the marketplace to my pedigree or scholastic success. Not that there is anything wrong with education. I encourage it. But my secret sauce has simply been my ability to stop, listen and meditate when the Holy Spirit gives me supernatural downloads that exceed human understanding.

That morning, I asked God to give me a deep understanding of the "supersonic" message. I felt led to look up Scriptures about earthquakes in the Bible. And that is when the hair on my arms stood at attention and I saw the first supersonic shockwave ever recorded.

> And when Jesus had cried out again in a loud voice, he gave up his spirit.
> At that moment the curtain of the temple was torn in two from top to bottom. *The earth shook, the rocks split and the tombs broke open.* The bodies of many holy people who had died were raised to life.
>
> Matthew 27:50–52, emphasis added

Something beyond human understanding happened that day when Jesus said *yes!* to His Father and submitted to a willingness to do anything to fulfill His greater purpose. When He gave up His spirit, the earth quaked and the veil was torn. Satan thought he had won the ultimate victory and was probably having a party with his fellow demons as they sat back and laughed at the persecution, degradation and crucifixion of his archrival.

Where was God during the violation of His Son? Why didn't He stop the process and rescue His beloved child? Have you ever been falsely accused or suffered through shame and sorrow? Have you ever felt abandoned, rejected, abused or violated? Those were just a few of the emotions that were hanging on the cross that day when Satan thought his enemy was defeated. But the story was not over yet. The ultimate victory was on its way.

Jesus' spirit was so powerful it broke the sound barrier with the intensity of a Mach 25-plus reentry boom. When His spirit left His body, the earth quaked and the veil was torn. Jesus was the first to B.O.O.M. (break out of mediocrity) and shake off the cloak of humanity that was placed upon Him. When He rose from the grave, the earth quaked again. And another BOOM! took place, and all who were asleep were raised from their graves. Neither the earth nor the grave were powerful enough to contain Him.

Where did that power come from to raise Jesus and those who slept from their graves?

From the Holy Spirit.

As the disciples gathered together in perfect unity, harmony and oneness, fire from heaven fell: "The place where they were meeting *was shaken*. And they were all filled with the Holy Spirit and spoke the word of God boldly" (Acts 4:31, emphasis added). BOOM! happened again. This time it was so we might live with the same power of the Holy Spirit to step out of our mediocre mindsets and become the powerful agents of change God has destined us to be. Suddenly, the same power that raised Jesus from the dead now lived inside every believer.

Seat belt still on? Good. Because later that same day is when I finally watched *Wonder Woman*. There is a scene in the movie when her enemies are pressing in on her and her people, and instead of cowering in fear, she crosses her arms and bows her head and that is when a supersonic shockwave goes out of her body and annihilates her enemies for miles. When I watched that scene of the movie, something was triggered inside me as if an awakening was taking place. I cried as I envisioned myself as the leading character, fueled by the fire of the Holy Spirit with a supernatural power on earth. I felt a shift inside my heart take place and a courage overwhelm my being. I left the movie ready to embrace anything God might call me to do, even if it meant going where others had been unwilling to go and doing what others were unwilling to do.

While *Wonder Woman*, the movie, gave zero credit to God for the power she possessed, I am confident that true empowerment comes from the Holy Spirit and fuels us with a fire that defies impossibilities.

As a believer, you are not of this world. You have been given a supernatural, supersonic power to overcome darkness. You are to be in this world, but not of this world (see John 17:14–16). You, too, are called to BOOM!—break out of mediocrity.

Imagining yourself as a superhero is often difficult due to the incredible pressures you face as a woman on any given day. Every woman faces inner voices that tell her she is not good enough, qualified or capable of changing the world in any way. Whether in business, family relationships or everyday life, those gnarly voices of defeat come to kill, steal and destroy your God-given power and influence.

Once the Holy Spirit empowers you, however, everything changes. You may feel less than qualified, the least likely to succeed or over-whelmed with the pressures of life. You may have dirty diapers piling up that keep you grounded in thoughts of mediocrity. Perhaps you are surrounded by people who remind you of your limitations. But the pressures of life are actually what create our greatest pearls of wisdom. And here is one other interesting fact about supersonic booms. They can only take place when an immense amount of air pressure is placed around a fast-moving object.

The pressure produces the BOOM!

Likewise, when you embrace your God-given superpowers, you have the potential to turn the dynamic tension of circumstances around you into creative solutions that birth new companies, launch nonprofit organizations, overturn broken policies and influence nations.

Through this book, you are about to embark on a fast-moving journey that helps you turn the pressures of your life into supersonic power that the Holy Spirit can use to put you in places of influence so that your voice, your life and your story can change the world.

Are you ready for a new alter ego that allows you to become more than you thought you could be? If so, then strap on your cape, draw your sword and position your crown. You are about to learn how to win over your adversaries, silence your inner critic and bust out of your comfort zone to become the woman of strength, influence and power you were destined to be.

part one

UNLEASHING YOUR INNER SUPERHERO

unleash (verb):
: to free from or as if from a leash
: let loose; to throw, shoot
or set in motion forcefully[1]

1

Satan's Kryptonite

She was small in stature and quiet in nature, but her prayers penetrated the heavens.

I was born in Dallas, Texas, to very young parents. My mom was seventeen and my dad was eighteen when they married. They met when they were only twelve and thirteen. As young as they were, they had great faith and a deep desire to be used by God to do something significant in the world. My grandfather was the pastor of a church in the South Oak Cliff community of Dallas. My dad played the piano at church and directed the choir while my mom played the organ.

When I was only eighteen months old, my parents faced the painful reality that I was a very sick little girl. What seemed to be a cold turned into pneumonia. Doctors were concerned because they could not seem to make the symptoms go away. After continuous bouts of pneumonia and many tests, our family doctor diagnosed me with cystic fibrosis, a lung disease that, at that time, was incurable and deadly.

Receiving such a devastating report would cause some parents to fall into a state of anxiety or great fear. But my parents had a clear revelation about God's power to heal, and they knew it was not a doctor or a diagnosis that had the final say in my destiny on earth. They recognized the enemy's role in trying to snuff out my life and stood their ground in defending my body against the spirit of infirmity that was trying to take me out. Instead of repeating the diagnosis, they put on their "It's not over till I win" mentality and began to pray. That was the only thing they knew to do, especially when the doctors had issued such a devasting diagnosis.

Next, they called on other faith-filled leaders, pastors and ministers to agree with them for a miracle from God. They asked everyone to pray these words as if my life depended on them: "She will live and not die, and she will proclaim the Good News of Christ to the nations." They refused to accept the report of disease over my body, and instead, they stood on the Word of God with a certainty in God's healing power that outweighed the diagnosis. Their brazen faith remained unshaken as they aligned their words with the truth of God's Word.

Following that prayer vigil, the cough subsided and the lung congestion cleared up. After a few weeks, they took me back to the doctor, who gladly reported that symptoms of cystic fibrosis were completely gone. Of course, the doctors assumed they might return. From that day forward, however, I never had another sign of pneumonia, cystic fibrosis, asthma or any other dysfunction of my lungs. How amazing that the enemy tries to destroy us in the very place God intends to use us to impact the world!

God had a plan to turn those broken lungs into a brazen voice of hope, help and healing to nations. Soon, the weakness diagnosed as lung disease was replaced with a powerful high-pitched squeal my parents said was most obnoxious when my older brother would merely touch me or annoy me in some unforeseen way. But instead of letting the annoying screams frustrate them, my parents saw the annoyance as a miracle in progress.

My vocal power and lung capacity eventually developed into a five-and-a-half-octave singing voice that would open doors for me to sing and speak on stages around the world with five U.S. presidents and declare God as the miracle worker in my life. And the same power that flowed through my body back then is equally available to heal today, for "Jesus Christ is the same yesterday and today and forever" (Hebrews 13:8).

Prayer, the "Secret Sauce"

> Take the helmet of salvation and the sword of the Spirit, which is the word of God. *And pray in the Spirit* on all occasions with all kinds of prayers and requests. With this in mind, be alert and always keep on praying for all the Lord's people.
>
> Ephesians 6:17–18, emphasis added

If you are familiar with the DC comic book universe, then you know that kryptonite is the one weakness of the otherwise-indestructible Superman. Kryptonite is composed of radiactive particles that come from Superman's original home planet, Krypton.

Some try to paint Superman as a Christ figure, but this one weakness leaves Superman as more of a wannabe than a true Savior of the world. God has no weaknesses or limitations, nor does He know failure. He cannot lie and He always wins. The Holy Spirit who lives in you is God's all-powerful, all-knowing and all-consuming fire.

Unlike God, Satan has weaknesses that are easily penetrated when we study his history and his kryptonite. Faith, love, joy, peace, patience, generosity, forgiveness and, yes, prayer are heaven's currency, as well as Satan's kryptonite—his Achilles' heel, weak spot or chink in his armor. BOOM! There it is—the secret sauce revealed.

*Prayer is to Satan what kryptonite was to
Superman; it weakens his defenses against you.*

Prayer that is grounded in faith and rooted in love changes things. Prayer works. Even science has proven the power of prayer, and some of the world's most prestigious schools continue to study its effects. Prayer destroys the work of the enemy against your life. It is the umbilical cord between you and God and the key to bringing the power of heaven to earth. When you add the prayer of faith to your arsenal in the workplace and in your family, you will begin to see massive transformation take place and miracles will manifest. But before we dive deep into understanding the power or fire of the Holy Spirit, it is essential to fully know the significance of spirit-to-Spirit communication or prayer.

Prayer is not some mystical incantation or prescribed mantra of religion. Instead, it is the way you build a relationship with God, share your gratitude with Him and voice your needs or concerns. At the very basic level, prayer is talking with God during your day and getting His advice on how to live. Adam and Eve had a perfect relationship with God in the Garden of Eden. They walked with God, talked with Him and perfectly managed the marketplace God had given them. He showed them how to steward the many animals, plants and trees, as well as how to multiply their harvest so they could live in complete abundance. In this perfect communion with God, they lacked nothing.

Satan cringed at the thought that mankind could have the same intimacy with God that he had been stripped of for an eternity. When Satan used his crafty wickedness against Adam and Eve to manipulate their focus, his intent was to break up the perfect union between heaven and earth. When Eve ate of the one forbidden fruit and Adam followed in her footsteps, sin entered the world, creating a canyon of separation between God and man. Prior to that separation, Adam and Eve conversed with God in total agreement, and God responded in absolute oneness and harmony.

Heaven and Earth Collide

The Old Testament books of the Bible describe how God created a process of redemption that would bridge the massive divide between heaven and earth, God and man. For centuries, the blood of sacrificed animals was used as a way to cover sin and bring humans into right relationship with God. Can you imagine if that was our practice today and our only way of reconnecting with God? Animal activists would be in an uproar. But thanks be to God, He offered an even better plan. God chose to send His Son from heaven as a perfect Lamb to be the "once and for all" sacrifice for mankind.

"For God so loved the world, that He gave His only begotten Son, that whoever believes in Him shall not perish, but have eternal life" (John 3:16 NASB). Jesus is the spotless Lamb who was sacrificed on a cross for the sins of all those who call on His name and open their hearts to the Father. But God was not just interested in forgiving our sins. He wanted to empower us to live with victory, dominion and authority over Satan in our everyday lives. And that is why He also sent us His Spirit. The Holy Spirit of God was sent to live in us and equip us with the mindset, skill sets and authority to overpower the works of the enemy.

Direct Connect

Today, one of the most effective ways to build great business or interpersonal relationships is through collaboration and open communication.

In the same way, prayer is simply communicating and collaborating with God with great transparency of heart. In an instant, you can have a direct connect with the Creator of the universe. Tapping in to God's mainframe through prayer opens your mind and emotions to limitless possibilities, wisdom, power and potential. Praying spirit to Spirit with God should be a powerful part of your offensive strategy for success in all things.

In Luke 7:22 (MSG) Jesus said,

"Go back and tell John what you have just seen and heard:
    The blind see,
    The lame walk,
    Lepers are cleansed,
    The deaf hear,
    The dead are raised,
    The wretched of the earth have God's salvation hospitality extended to them."

Even today Jesus chooses ordinary people just like you and me as conduits for His miracles when we allow ourselves to be used by God in an extraordinary way. When Jesus' disciples questioned the authenticity of His resurrection and whether or not they, too, could do what Jesus did, look at what He told them:

"Believe me: I am in my Father and my Father is in me. If you can't believe that, believe what you see—these works. The person who trusts me will not only do what I'm doing but even greater things, because I, on my way to the Father, am giving you the same work to do that I've been doing. You can count on it. From now on, whatever you request along the lines of who I am and what I am doing, I'll do it. That's how the Father will be seen for who he is in the Son. I mean it. Whatever you request in this way, I'll do."

John 14:11–14 MSG

The Power of Agreement

Prayer is powerful, but the prayer of agreement is impenetrable. The word *agreement* means "harmony of opinion, action, or character"[1] (in other words, the absence of incompatibility). If you really want to wage war on the darkness around you in your home, the marketplace or anywhere that you see change necessary, find someone who will stand in agreement and perfect alignment with your prayers. When times come, and they will, when you need allied forces, remember these words Jesus spoke to His disciples when He showed the keys to breaking through chains of addiction and bondage to sin: "Again, truly I tell you that if two of you on earth *agree about anything they ask for*, it will be done for them by my Father in heaven. For where two or three gather in my name, there am I with them" (Matthew 18:19–20, emphasis added).

In this passage, Jesus was talking about how to restore people in the marketplace and how to help people break free from the things in life that hold them back from heaven's best. He was showing His disciples that sometimes they need to team up in prayer and create an even more powerful source through the prayer of agreement. Notice verse 9 says that if two people can *"agree* about anything that they ask for . . ."* (emphasis added). In other words, two people must be in perfect agreement with one another on the specific prayer request they are putting before the Lord. This means they are now approaching the throne of God in perfect alignment—they are praying for the exact same thing with unified hearts.

Too many marriages fail in this area due to discord, division, anger and misalignment in their prayers. They pray, but then their unity is broken with discord, rendering the prayer impotent. Satan loves it when Christians disagree or spouses argue. Why? Because he knows it eliminates the power of kryptonite (prayer) to stop his attacks.

Prayer Blockers

The enemy loathes the prayer of agreement. He knows his attacks are sabotaged when God's people dwell together in unity. That is why he throws fiery arrows to divide us from those around us. Here are five of the most common prayer blockers the enemy uses to hinder our prayers.

1. Unbelief

But when you ask, you must believe and not doubt, because the one who doubts is like a wave of the sea, blown and tossed by the wind. That person should not expect to receive anything from the Lord. Such a person is double-minded and unstable in all they do.

James 1:6–8

Unbelief is a thief that steals the potency of our prayers. When we doubt God or fail to have faith in His promises, we block the power of our prayers. Stress, worry, confusion and frustration with others all prove a lack of faith.

2. Unforgiveness

"And when you stand praying, if you hold anything against anyone, forgive them, so that your Father in heaven may forgive you your sins."

Mark 11:25

Holding grudges against others not only separates us from that person but creates separation between us and God. Whether in marriage or at work or in any area of our lives, unforgiveness is a weapon of the enemy to keep us from having perfect access to God's miracle-working power. This is vital. Prayer will not work without forgiveness.

3. Strife

Where envy and self-seeking exist, confusion and every evil thing are there.

James 3:16 NKJV

Though most often a sign of unforgiveness, strife also hinders our prayer life. Strife is merely acting on unforgiveness and choosing to put force behind our disappointment in others. When we allow strife to divide us from our spouse or other Christians, we partner with Satan's plan against us. The absence of strife is the key to eliminating the evil work of the enemy.

4. Disobedience

If I regard iniquity in my heart, the Lord will not hear me.

Psalm 66:18 AMPC

If the prayer of faith is Satan's kryptonite, disobedience to God's Word is ours. When we know what to do and yet choose not to do it, we are in direct disobedience to God, and this hinders our prayers and weakens our battle plan. If we have been enlightened to God's truth and know His Word, yet consistently choose to turn our back on it, we are missing the mark of His *best* for our lives.

Behold, the LORD's hand is not shortened, that it cannot save; neither his ear heavy, that it cannot hear: But your iniquities have separated between you and your God, and your sins have hid his face from you, that he will not hear.

Isaiah 59:1–2 KJV

The word *sin* is a simple archery term used when an arrow missed the bull's-eye. Upon impact, the scout at the target would yell, "Sin!" signifying that the bull's-eye had been missed. To sin against God means we have missed the mark of obedience, and when sin becomes a habit, it turns into a foothold.

5. Idolatry

When we put anything above God, we create idols of false worship. This is a guaranteed way to block the supernatural flow of heaven's full power being unleashed on earth. Many people question whether or not God still performs miracles on earth today simply because miracles are not as prevalent as in the days of Jesus. But instead of saying that God has changed, which He does *not* (see Hebrews 13:8), could it be that we have changed and taken on idols of worship that hinder our prayers? Could it be that we have allowed the things of this world—the technologies, accolades, hunger for fame or search for approval—to become more important than God Himself?

The first Commandment reads, "Thou shalt have no other gods before me" (Exodus 20:2 KJV). In the days of Hosea, Israel was living in complete sin, openly displaying their pagan worship through their self-indulging celebrations. Despite their claiming to be deeply religious and dedicated to temple worship, God rebuked them harshly.

> "Listen to this, priests! Attention, people of Israel! Royal family—give me your ears! You're in charge of justice around here. But what have you done? Exploited people at Mizpah, ripped them off on Tabor, victimized them at Shittim. I'm going to punish the lot of you.
>
> "I know you, Ephraim, inside and out. Yes, Israel, I see right through you! Ephraim, you've played your sex-and-religion games long enough. All Israel is thoroughly polluted. They couldn't turn to God if they wanted to. Their evil life is a bad habit. Every breath they take is a whore's breath. They wouldn't recognize GOD if they saw me.
>
> "Bloated by arrogance, big as a house, they're a public disgrace, the lot of them—Israel, Ephraim, Judah—lurching and weaving down their guilty streets. When they decide to get their lives together and go off looking for GOD once again, they'll find it's too late. I, GOD, will be long gone. They've played fast and loose with me for too long, filling the country with their bastard offspring. A plague of locusts will devastate their violated land."
>
> Hosea 5:1–7 MSG

God is very clear that we can have massive success, be notable figures, parade behind massive churches, build impressive buildings and even rise to the status of a nation of global power, but if we are rich with idol worship, we will be poor with the things of God, including miracles, signs and wonders and the powerful manifestations that come as proof of the Holy Spirit's presence.

God has proven time and time again that if a nation does not turn away from idol worship and seek His face, He will shake the nation and level the playing field. He will cause systems to cease and kingdoms to fall in order to capture the heart of His people. We see this through the many plagues, pestilence, pressures, imprisonments and pilgrimages throughout the Bible. God will ultimately shake the earth before He will let the enemy conquer His people.

Prayer is our way back to God, and the key to answered prayer is to fall on our faces in humility and turn our hearts back into a whole and right relationship with God, our Father. The key to answered prayer is to fall on our faces in humility and turn our hearts back into a whole and right relationship with God, our Father. "If my people, which are called by my name, shall humble themselves, and pray, and seek my face, and turn from their wicked ways; then will I hear from heaven, and will forgive their sin, and will heal their land" (2 Chronicles 7:14 KJV).

The Holy Spirit *in* You

Once Jesus returned to His place at the right hand of God in heaven, He sent the Holy Spirit of God not only to be with us but to live *in* us so that once again we could have perfect union with God (see John 14:15–17). Consequently, you can talk to God, walk with God, go to work with God and even take vacations with the Holy Spirit of God in every step you take.

Prayer is a dialogue that is as natural as the conversations you have with your dearest friends, family, pastor or colleagues. The Holy Spirit of God is not far off in heaven somewhere; He is in you and with you 24/7. You do not have to be restricted by only going to a priest, pastor or earthly advisor to connect with God. Although those ministerial leaders serve great purpose in equipping us, you can walk and talk with the Creator of the universe about *anything* at any time, in any place you choose.

Prayer is the key to sabotaging the work of the enemy in your life. Prayer is your access to God, and His Holy Spirit is your portal to bringing heaven to earth. As you continue through the rest of this book, you are going to step into advanced weapons and strategies that will empower you and fully *unleash* in you the miracle-working, life-changing power of God that you now have access to through the Holy Spirit.

BOOM!—TIME TO REFLECT

You have the potential to be a human pipeline of heaven-to-earth communications. When you stand in right relationship with God, you can become a conduit of His power and limitless potential. Stop for a moment and consider if there is anything in your heart that would hinder a perfect flow of God's miracle-working power in and through your life. What prayer blockers do you need to eliminate from your relationships, life and business?

Pray this prayer out loud:

Dear heavenly Father,
I believe that You sent Your Son, Jesus, to die on the cross for my sins and to fill the gap of separation between us. I want intimacy with You. I want to know You. I want to walk and talk with You daily. I want to know Your voice, hear Your truth and obey Your every command. Invade my heart, O God, and cleanse me even of my secret sins. I repent and turn toward You now, in Jesus' name, Amen.

2

Warriors in Training

She was a sinner; He saw a saint. She was a pagan; He saw a queen.

When I was a little girl, I was wimpy and whiny, and people often called me a sissy. It may be hard to believe, but there was a time when I was timid and shy. A shift of courage started for me in fourth grade, however, when I began to desire affirmation like most other fourth graders. When our school announced auditions were being held for the school musical, *Cinderella*, being a fairly good singer, I auditioned for the lead role. I practiced my audition piece daily, dreaming of being Cinderella. At night, I would lie in my bed and imagine being swept off my feet by Prince Charming, who would whisk me away into a magnificent castle.

When the announcement was made on who was cast into the various roles, I was stunned. The theatre teacher did not see me as the Cinderella type. Instead, she cast me in the role of the ugly stepsister named Anastasia. I cried and felt defeated. The following year, I went out for the lead role of the young lad in *The Jungle Book*. Instead of getting the lead, I was chosen to be King Louie, the hairy gorilla. I viewed it as another setback. Clearly, I saw my-self differently than how the teacher saw me. I realized for the first time in my life that other people will try to define who they think you are, and if you let it, their perception can become your reality.

That same year, I also told my parents I wanted to play basket-ball, even though I was skinny, scrawny and the shortest girl trying out for the team. There was no way I had the physical attributes to be successful. I was potentially setting myself up for another failure. I asked my father what he thought. Despite my limitations, he saw an opportunity to turn my fearful nature into fearless courage. He said, "Honey, if you're going to play that sport, you will have to work harder than all of the other girls to compensate for your size."

Just because I had enough determination to overcome my phys-ical limitations and had the encouragement of my parents did not mean it was easy. At first, getting the ball up high enough to touch the rim of the goal was a struggle. But I refused to quit. Thankfully, the coach put everyone on the team who tried out, so I at least made the team, even if I had to sit on the bench for most of the year. When the rare occasion came when I got to play, it was usually because we were winning by twenty points or more.

My jersey was so long it covered my shorts, as if I were wearing a dress. When I got another player to pass me the ball finally, I had to stop and use a "granny shot," which is putting the ball between my legs and throwing it underhand toward the rim. It was the only way I could get it high enough to touch the rim.

While I desperately wanted to hear the cheers of my peers screaming in amazement at my skills, all I heard was people laugh-ing at me. I was too small, too inexperienced and too weak to make a notable impact. No doubt, I was swinging for the fences, but I kept coming up short—literally.

Depression started to creep in. I began thinking I was not good at anything. Soon, I began to fear failure and wanted to stop trying to reach big goals. I was starving for affirmation but kept facing rejection. Just as I saw myself as Cinderella, I saw myself as a superstar basketball player. Others did not see me that way. Slowly but surely their views were becoming my own. That fear started to paralyze me and could have kept me in a prison of self-doubt my whole life.

But I was one of the very few and truly blessed little girls to have a mom and dad who refused to let me quit. Instead, they quoted Scriptures to encourage me. Things like, "Honey, God has not given you a spirit of fear, but of power, love, and of a sound mind."[1] Determined to raise a winner and not a whiner, they proceeded to paint the picture of how much God loved me and how valuable I was to Him. They also clued me in on the fact that there was also a real enemy who wanted to silence my voice and wanted to defeat me.

My parents boldly declared, "Staci, God has a plan and a purpose for your life, and Satan does not want your voice to be heard. You must determine in your heart that you will never give up, let up or shut up till God takes you up to heaven. You are destined to win. You have the Spirit of God living inside of you. You can do anything He has called you to do."

God unleashed me from a spirit of fear, and I was filled with His Holy Spirit. Though I was young, a new fire burned in my belly. That did not mean my limitations went away. I just realized I could either let life decide which opportunities I would receive, or I could begin to hone my skills in order to increase my odds.

The Power of the Holy Spirit

> I have fought the good fight, I have finished the race, I have kept the faith.
>
> 2 Timothy 4:7

One day, my dad was watching me sit the bench at a basketball game. I could tell by the look on his face he was a bit worried.

After the game, one in which I failed to do anything of significance, he sat me down and said, "Staci, I will never say you can't do something in life. I want you to always believe that anything is possible. However, if your heart is set on basketball, you are going to have to work harder, longer and give more effort to developing your skills than every other player on that court."

At that moment, I let his words sink in and made the decision to do whatever was necessary to overcome my size. Determined to develop extraordinary ball-handling skills and an outside shot that would even rival the boys, I practiced shooting the ball every day after school for hours. I drew lines on our driveway to practice my ball-handling skills. Basketball became my life. I even started imagining what it would be like to be the first white girl on the Harlem Globetrotters. I became relentless in doing my best to make that dream a reality. I lived and breathed basketball.

The next year came, and while I made the basketball team, I learned quickly that if you are the skinniest, shortest and weakest player on the team, you cannot let anything slide. I had to muster up the grit to work harder and longer and play smarter than everyone else on the court. I did not know it then, but those disappointments, setbacks and voices of mocking laughter, though painful, were grooming me to be a powerhouse woman of resilient courage in the future. They were sharpening my resolve and helping me take hits like a heavyweight champion of the world.

My dad deserves a lot of credit. His relentless coaching and encouragement, along with hours of practice, turned my weakness into a powerful strength that would set my entire future up for victory. It was a long time between being cast as Anastasia and seeing my season of success on the basketball court come to fruition, but I refused to quit. As my confidence grew, instead of being broken by the opposition, I became a tough little scrapper—a little princess warrior ready for battle.

Having an older brother also helped. I remember being outside of our house day after day, trying to get three shots to go in the goal before I would let myself go inside. My brother, who was over six feet tall, asked if I wanted to shoot some hoops with him. While I loved playing ball with him, we usually ended up in a fight because I wanted to win so badly.

One day we were playing a game of one-on-one, and he beat me with very little chance of me even getting possession of the ball. I could not even make one point against him. He started to walk away as if I was not even worth the effort. I shouted, "No! Let's play again!" He came back, only to beat me again. I begged him to let me have another try, and that time I scored a goal. He rubbed my head and said, "Sorry, Sis. Maybe tomorrow!" I grabbed his T-shirt, held on for dear life and cried, "No, Bubba. Please play again. It's not over till I win!"

"It's not over till I win!"

That moment triggered an inner strength that superseded my outer weaknesses. My father's consistent words of affirmation further deepened my resolve to win: "You can do it, baby. Just don't give up. You can do all things through Christ who gives you strength."[2] Looking back now, I can see his words were watering seeds of greatness in my heart and the desire to be more than I thought I could be. Instead of being broken by defeat, I became a tenacious bulldog, hungry to latch onto something and refuse to let go till I got it. The more my parents encouraged me to embrace the power of the Holy Spirit's role in my life, the more I began to believe I was unstoppable.

I began winning awards and breaking records in basketball due to my willingness to work hard and pay a price that other girls were unwilling to pay. I gave up parties, movies, any interest in the opinion of boys and other activities to practice my skills on the basketball court. Soon, my ball-handling skills and outside shots set me up to average 23 to 28 points per game and enabled me to be selected for the Junior Olympics.

Looking back, I can see how the Holy Spirit was meeting me at the point of my willingness to hone the skills God had given me. The more I believed I could do anything, the more nothing seemed impossible. Soon, I became hooked on winning, and for the next thirty years of my life, my drive to succeed became my drug of choice. No matter what the challenge, come hell or high water, I was going to win. That was the birth of an addiction to approval. My need to win became a self-gratifying need to lead, to get recognition, to be verbally affirmed by others. The more people said attagirl, the more I felt approved.

My pursuit of significance was equally fed daily by my willingness to work, work, work. And while my drive to win birthed a relentless work ethic within me, I would soon realize that no matter how many accolades I achieved, enough was never enough. I began to believe that my worth or values were only tallied when I had big wins, new awards or achievements that the world would appreciate. Soon, my inner value was buried beneath a need to please others and an addiction to the adrenaline of success.

The Fire of the Holy Spirit

While the above story is a positive take on how to become relentless in overcoming adversity, I have since learned from that experience that winning for personal approval or applause will never be enough. And that is not why God has given us the fire of the Holy Spirit.

Today, self-help coaches and business gurus are all the craze. We are taught that in order to gain power or worth, we must look better, appear younger, work harder, blend in and even give up our family in pursuit of our dreams for success—all of this for the goal of achieving success according to the world's standards. Social media persuades us to search for acceptance through greater achievements, accolades and social efforts to win the favor of the world. But enough is never enough, and the thirst for greatness in the human battle of ego will never be quenched.

By contrast, God does not look at "value" the way we do. He sees beyond the confines of this world, instead viewing us from the perspective of spiritual impact potential. Here is what I mean: In my hands, a tennis racquet may be worth $250. Put that same racquet in the hands of Serena Williams, and it could be worth $171 million or more. A football in my hands is only worth around $75, but in the hands of Peyton Manning, it might be worth $230 million. And in my hands, a basketball worth around $100 has a potential value of over $275 million in the hands of LeBron James.

Serena Williams, Peyton Manning and Lebron James all have extraordinary God-given talent. And they worked hard to develop that talent, which has turned into fame and fortune. Self-effort and achievement, however, while celebrated by the world, are not the end goal in God's currency.

What am I saying? In our own efforts, our life is only worth what our *effort* or grind can produce. We work hard, toil, practice, stretch and strive for greatness. Often, that might mean more profits but less peace. When we put our life and our story in the hands of God, however, we move out of our natural abilities alone and allow the Creator of the universe to mold us into a priceless treasure worth far more than money could ever buy.

Moses parted the Red Sea with the power of God. His talent did not produce those results. Nor did his hard work or immense amount of staff-holding practice create such a magnificent outcome. Instead, in that moment heaven broke through into humanity, defying the laws of the universe, to produce something supernatural.

No matter how hard athletes train, they can never gain that much strength or ability. Regardless of how much you study, exercise, set goals, attend self-help conferences or practice your skills, you can never achieve as much as you can through the power of the Holy Spirit working through your life. This is the secret of being fueled by fire. It is greater than being fueled by extraordinary talent, beauty or skill. It is supernatural.

If Jesus looked you in the eyes today, what would He see? You might be surprised to know that He sees a warrior just waiting to be trained and a woman ready for greatness.

BOOM!—TIME TO REFLECT

Take a moment and reflect upon your own life. What happened in your history that shaped your identity and how you seek approval? Have you ever felt that no matter how hard you work or how much you do for others, it never seems to be enough? Describe a memory that has impacted your need for affirmation. Then pray this prayer:

Father God,

I know there is more to life that what I've been experiencing, and I want everything You have for me. I know that my life, in my own hands, will never compare to my life and talents when placed under Your control. I surrender my life, and I invite the power of the Holy Spirit to fuel my passions from this day forward. I am ready to do what You ask me to do, knowing it's not over till we win!

3

Running to Win

"Run, girl, run! This is your race to win!"

I love a good underdog movie. One of my favorites is *Secretariat*, the comeback story of common housewife and mom Penny Chenery, played by Diane Lane. Despite her lack of experience, she agrees to take over the management of her family's thoroughbred farm after her father becomes ill. Before his passing, he looks at her and says, "Run your race!" With relentless courage and tenacity, she forges her way through the male-dominated world of horse racing to foster a gifted colt that ultimately defied the odds and crossed the finish line as the Triple Crown winner of 1973.

When I was eighteen years old, I entered a contest with 8,900 other singers in Canada. The prize was that the winner would perform a solo at the opening and closing ceremonies of the Olympics, working with the famed producer David Foster. My aunt entered me by sending in a video of my singing on a little local TV show. When I received the call to come to Toronto, Canada, to compete as a finalist, I was thrilled, honored and scared silly since I had never traveled alone or been away from my family for extended periods of time. They narrowed the selection down to the top ten, and I flew with the other contestants to sing privately for David Foster and a panel of celebrity judges. I remember how scared I was, knowing I was competing against professional opera stars, recording artists and other highly trained vocalists.

The day of my final audition, I called my mom and dad crying. "I can't do this," I said. "Like literally, I learned the audition song in the wrong octave. All of the other singers are singing in a higher key that is completely outside of my range."

Hearing the fear in my voice, my father said, "Honey, God has positioned you in that room 'for such a time as this.' Stop looking at the other singers and get your eyes on the One who has brought you to this place. Don't sing like them. Sing like God has uniquely trained you to sing." I will never forget his parting words of encouragement. After they prayed for peace to sweep over my heart and guard my mind, my dad said, "Baby, you weren't born to sing opera. You were born to sing from your soul with passion and grit. You sing like *you*. Look those judges in the eye with boldness and let God's strength and power be your source. The Holy Spirit will fill the gap!"

And so, I walked into the audition room with David Foster and a panel of judges and sang, I mean, *sang* that song as if I were singing the national anthem on the Fourth of July. I sang with passion, grit, sincerity and boldness. When I finished, the room sat silent. David Foster leaned forward and said, "Do it again."

My hands shook as I sang it a second time. Then a sudden peace swept over me as I connected with the judges in a deep way. David Foster leaned over and whispered something to the other judges. I kept looking them in the eyes and compassionately singing the chorus to the song "Can't You Feel It?" by David Foster. When I did, something shifted in the room. In that moment, chills spread all over my body as I realized God did not want me to be a copycat of the talents of others. He did not bring me to that room to blend in; He uniquely gifted me to be different and stand out.

And He empowered me to connect with others in a supernatural way when I allowed His peace to transcend my understanding (see Philippians 4:7).

I believe the Holy Spirit took my natural talent that day and anointed it with supernatural power that allowed me to stand out as the voice for the 1988 Olympics. I won the competition and was blessed to sing under the torch that year in front of the entire world.

You Are Destined to Win

> In a race everyone runs, but only one person gets first prize. So run your race to win.
>
> 1 Corinthians 9:24 TLB

Superheroes win. They may have to endure epic battles and face formidable opponents, but in the end, they always win. No matter what they face or how many villains they must conquer, the end of the story is always the same: Superheroes *win*.

But most women never recognize this hidden power, nor have they known how to use it as a weapon of warfare in everyday life. Instead, they rely solely on their human efforts, talents or intellect to grind through the many obstacles of life as they climb the proverbial ladder of success. To some women, *winning* is not a word they would use to describe their life. In fact, for many the idea of someone "winning" often stirs up traumatic memories of suffering at the hands of a narcissistic leader. Or perhaps it triggers memories of sexual abuse, domestic violence, shame or failure.

If you have been dominated by men or women who have put you down or held you back in any way, you may live in a prison of emotional pain that has silenced your voice and harnessed your full potential. If you have ever tried to accomplish something and failed, you may have stopped trying to conquer the battles God has destined you to win. Right now, you may not feel like a superhero, but the day you invited the Holy Spirit into your life, you took on a new nature that is superinfused with a firepower that has the potential to shift circumstances beyond your control in a dramatic way.

In the pages of this book, you will discover a better way to establish your rule and reign on earth. You will learn how to activate the hidden power of the Holy Spirit within you to become a force of change in the world around you. You are about to win with a landslide of divinely orchestrated advantages set in your favor.

My Papaw used to tell me the story of a young boy who was going fishing and caught grasshoppers for bait that he put in a jar. The grasshoppers jumped with wild fury, hoping to escape the jar they had been confined to. The little boy watched them closely, and after an hour they were only jumping sporadically. But then they stopped jumping altogether. Having hit the lid repeatedly in their attempted escape, the grasshoppers grew to believe that freedom was impossible. The boy unscrewed the lid, and to his amazement the grasshoppers did not jump out, nor did they try to fly away. They had become conditioned to believe that even with the lid to their freedom fully removed, they could never escape.

Perhaps you have grown to be like those grasshoppers, and you have stopped trying to live the life of your dreams. Maybe there was a day when you had big dreams, visions, ideas of a happy life, a blissful family, a successful career, a pure relationship or abundant finances. But as time passed and opposition seemingly held you back, you stopped trying as hard. Maybe you have even settled for a life that is "good enough" but certainly not all you dreamed it would be.

Girl, I am writing this book to shout lovingly, "Get up!" God is not finished with you yet, and this book is intended to remind you of just how powerful you really are. It is time to start jumping again. It is time to start dreaming again. It is time to start winning again. It is time to look up and believe that "He who has begun a good work in you will complete it" (Philippians 1:6 NKJV).

While many women have stopped trying to win due to past failures or opposition, today we also see a new insurgence of women who are hungry to win at all costs, forsaking motherhood, femininity, time with family and even their peace. Conforming to the world does not produce victory. I know the feeling of being addicted to an insatiable need for public approval and applause, and I spent nearly forty years of my life bound to a high-performance mentality. At first, this type of winning seems noble and even courageous, but when it becomes a life quest, this drive to win can evolve into an addiction where enough is never enough.

Maybe you have been programmed that to win, you must do more, be more or have more accolades in life to prove your worth. Perhaps the attention or awards you have received have come because of your talents, your looks, your pedigree, your cooking skills or even your "winning personality." The truth is that while those characteristics are good, they are not where your greatest superpower will come from. Whether you are reading this book from the filter of pain, ego, pride or pleasure, the truth is, you were destined to win. In its purest form, winning is a part of your inheritance as a follower of Christ. And how you win will determine the way in which you experience peace in the process.

Your Mission Field Awaits

> But thanks be to God! He gives us the victory through our Lord Jesus Christ.
>
> 1 Corinthians 15:57

We are surrounded by a distorted view of what it means to win as women today. Winning does not mean grinding through the workday in "beast mode" or dominating our peers by working ten times harder than those around us. To win, a woman does not have to trade in her skirt or femininity for fatigues and masculinity. Instead, God created woman with a supernatural power to influence others and make choices that lead to life, liberty and happiness. This power, as you will soon read, is best activated through humility, gentleness, kindness, generosity, wisdom, prudence and spiritual authority.

As soon as you believe in Jesus as the Son of God, you have won. You have the power to overcome the world. Jesus died and went to heaven to give you the free gift of the Holy Spirit to live on the inside of your spirit and help you do things that would otherwise be impossible on your own. It is as simple as sincerely saying, "Lord, I receive Your Spirit. I want everything You have for me." In that moment, a spiritual and supernatural shift takes place. You open the floodgates for heaven's firepower to rush into your life and transform you from the inside out.

I wrote *Fueled by Fire* to teach you how to tap into the fire of the Holy Spirit to help you rewrite the end of your superhero story with a supernatural ending. No matter what chapter you are in, you hold the pen that will write the end of your masterpiece. You can either stay focused on the battles of your past, or you can begin writing your comeback story today.

If you change your story, you change your life.

The end of your story does not have to end in bitterness, failure or defeat. You can learn how to be fueled by a power that supersedes your work, your family, your talents and your relationships. This fire will help you reshape your mind, rethink your relationships and rewrite the ending of your story as a superhero who leaves a winning legacy for her family, friends and community.

*Every woman has a story, and every
story can change the world.*

When a woman is truly unleashed by God and filled with the superpower of the Holy Spirit, her story begins to scare the hell out of the devil. It means that she is supernaturally loosed from the opinions of man and the emotions of her former sufferings. She is free from the need to toil for selfish ambitions and personal power and is, instead, fully surrendered to the Holy Spirit and willing to say yes to her mission of winning battles for Kingdom purposes.

Within each of us lies the potential to be the superhero our world needs today. No one would like a movie where the superhero does not win. No one goes to a blockbuster movie to watch a villain walk away with the plunder. Billions of dollars are spent each year to satisfy the human emotion of winning through superhero films like *Wonder Woman*, *Superman*, *The Avengers* and other movies where light conquers darkness. But often, for us as women, it is just a movie and we feel less than victorious when we go back to our real lives with real issues that really matter.

With the pressures of motherhood, expectations of family unity, emotions of aging, deadlines in business and the never-ending competition for power, few women would use the word *superhero* to describe themselves. But that is about to change.

What if you could suddenly be filled with a superpower that allows you to speak with boldness, overcome darkness, defy enemy opposition, see into the spirit realm and conquer evil with great courage? And what if you did not have to give up your femininity to do so?

While today's women's liberation movements speak of personal power, financial equality, transhuman conformity, ego-powered domination and self-choice as the narrative for power, you are about to see that God has a much different plan for the empowerment of women. God created woman to be brilliant, charming, influential, beautiful, gentle, wise and empowered with the secret sauce of heaven.

God wants to fill you with the power of the Holy Spirit to transform you into a superpowered human on earth, even as it is in heaven. He has a cape, a crown and a sword with your name on it, and now is the time for your inner superhero to arise.

The enemy fears the day you become the God-fearing Warrior Queen of boldness and significance you were destined to be. I assure you that the enemy of your destiny does *not* want you to finish this book, nor does he want you to recognize and fulfill your divine potential.

He could care less if you become successful, climb to the top of your game, gather a mass number of followers, be a notable speaker, make excessive amounts of money or experience fame and fortune. But what scares the *hell* out of him is when you awaken to God's highest purpose for your life, allowing the Holy Spirit of God to flow through you, empower your decisions and use your life and talents to penetrate the marketplace and make His name great in all the earth.

God wants to use your success for a much higher purpose. Let this book challenge your thought processes, engage your core values, awaken your wildest dreams, motivate your passions and empower you to step out of your comfort zone, and say yes to everything God has for your future. Your mission field, the marketplace, awaits you.

Let the great adventure begin!

BOOM!—TIME TO REFLECT

Have you ever asked for God to fill you with the fire of the Holy Spirit? I want to invite you to pray this prayer and receive everything God has in store for your life. When the Holy Spirit fills you to capacity, you will begin to see differently, think more courageously and want to be used for something greater than mediocrity. Are you ready?

Let's pray:

Father God,

I am just a girl, doing my best to make a difference in this world. But I realize that I can do nothing of great significance apart from You. I'm deeply sorry for the many mess-ups I've created in my life. I love You, and I want to serve You daily. I believe that You sent Jesus to die for my sins, and I accept that sacrifice over my life. Thank You for forgiving me, and fill me with Your Holy Spirit. I want to reflect You and be a source of Your power on earth. Thank You for this gift that I now receive. In Jesus' name, Amen.

4

Treasured Possessions

She looked at the abandoned crown, dusty and dated, and realized that what some call useless others call priceless.

When I was a little girl, I looked forward to going to garage sales with my mother. We loved rummaging through other people's junk, hoping to find our very own treasure. The truth is, we were always shopping for a bargain.

One Saturday, we saw a garage sale sign and made a quick stop. She gave me a quarter and told me I could buy anything I wanted. One table had a box full of junky old costume jewelry labeled "Ten Cents." Excited, I knew I would find a treasure. The box was full of beads and costume jewelry. A ring with black gunk all over it was at the bottom. It fit my finger and had a giant rock in it. I showed my mom, and she said, "Oh baby, let's not touch it until we get home and clean it up a bit." Little did I know that God was about to teach me a massive lesson on value.

When we got home, we put the treasured possession into a cup of dishwashing soap and let it soak while I got my bath. When I pulled the ring out of the nasty blackened water, it looked as good as new from the cleaning. Both my mom and I were amazed to discover that the ring was not a piece of junk after all. Instead, it was a beautiful fourteen-carat gold ring that held a giant topaz stone. The previous owner obviously did not know its worth because of the dirt and grime. Once in the hands of someone who would clean it up and give it some TLC, however, the dirt-covered ring became priceless.

God has continued to show me that lesson in leadership and life. No matter how successful we become, if our worth is not seen through the eyes of God's purposes, we will allow our emotions to corrode our worth and bury our potential. The enemy of our destiny comes to burden us with temptations, failure, rejection and sorrow so that, over time, we fail to recognize our intrinsic value. Instead of living the powerful lives of purpose God intended for us, we end up settling for a job, relationship or life that is less than God's best for us.

The cleansing process that God wants to take you through as a leader is a metamorphosis that transforms you into something more powerful and masterful than anything you could ever do yourself. Beneath every warrior is a child who, when surrendered to the hands of God, can become a fearless champion, ready for battle.

The purer the vessel, the greater the flow.

You, too, are a priceless treasure and quite possibly, you are still in the middle of God's process of preparing you, hardening, strengthening you and forging you through the potter's fire. Your ability to endure what you have already endured is proof that God is making something masterful out of your leadership and life. And yet, in the middle of the mess, it is not always easy to see what God is doing.

When our story appears to be a twisted pile of brokenness, emptiness, loneliness or unmet expectations, we can get frustrated and even depressed at times. When the laundry is piled up, the kids are fighting, the bills are overdue and the dog has gotten out for the twentieth time this year, it can be difficult to see yourself as a powerhouse of God, ready to take on the world.

Nevertheless, *don't quit*. God is creating a masterpiece in your very real, raw and relevant story. He is a master at taking ordinary people and turning them into extraordinary conduits of His power. If you let Him, He will turn your mess into a message that brings hope to those around you. But your story will never have full impact if you quit in the middle of the process of becoming all God has destined you to be.

Seedtime and Harvest

When I was growing up, my grandparents had a massive one-acre garden. I remember, as a little girl, watching them till the soil, then plant the seeds. I would help with the seed planting part and then find great joy when the first sprouts of harvest started to appear. I learned early on that seed planting day ("seedtime") and harvest day are two distinctly different moments in time. Everyone wants the harvest, but very few leaders are willing to stand the test of time.

Often, when we get a vision from God, we think that it should be delivered to us overnight. But just like the process of seed*time* . . . and harvest, our greatest days of impact will happen over the course of time and after the death, burial and spiritual resurrection of our egos. When a seed goes into the ground, it experiences a death process before new life can begin.

Jesus describes this transformational process like this:

"Listen carefully: Unless a grain of wheat is buried in the ground, dead to the world, it is never any more than a grain of wheat. But if it is buried, it sprouts and reproduces itself many times over. In the same way, anyone who holds on to life just as it is destroys that life. But if you let it go, reckless in your love, you'll have it forever, real and eternal."

John 12:24–25 MSG

As a marketplace leader, you will undoubtedly go through dark or quiet times of transition when it feels like God has forsaken you or pushed you aside. You may be in a place right now that feels like God has somehow forgotten you or the dreams in your heart. But don't you dare give up. God's not finished with you yet. The longer the preparation process, the greater the harvest ahead.

Don't give up. God is not finished with you yet.

One of the most powerful things about God's preparation process is how He redefines what is truly valuable in this life. Prior to his deep transformational shift, Paul was focused on titles, appearances and being a part of the elite social club of spiritual hierarchy. But that all changed the day Jesus appeared to him and changed his sight and perspective. Jesus said, "I am Jesus, whom you are persecuting" (Acts 9:5).

Think about how excited, and yet how restricted, Paul must have felt as a new believer. The disciples did not trust him, and the Jewish leaders wanted to kill him. He knew his conversion was authentic, but the world still could not see what Paul had seen. The seeds were planted in Paul, but a time of preparation in the back side of the desert was necessary before Paul's full release and public exposure.

The Quiet Season

He who began a good work in you is faithful to complete it and perfect it until the day of Christ.

Philippians 1:6

Over the years, anytime I have felt totally abandoned by friends, disrespected by peers, financially broken or falsely accused, I would find a quiet place and meditate on this one Scripture over and over and over again until it became my truth. At first, it was just words. But the more I meditated upon Philippians 1:6, the more I realized *God cannot lie*. And if He started my life, it is up to Him to perfect His work in me, turn my ashes into something beautiful (see Isaiah 61:3) and help me finish strong.

Every season of pain has been followed by a season of even greater power. Every setback during which it felt like God was abandoning me could eventually be seen as a setup for me to touch more lives. The cross you are currently carrying might very well be the one God uses to change the world with your story, in His timing.

This is the story behind my song "Cinderella, a Dream Come True." The song talks about a woman named Cinderella who is trapped in a mediocre life, feeling lost in the ashes of her past. While there is no fairy godmother or magic wand to change her situation, there is a God in whom all things are possible (see Matthew 19:26).

He is still in the business of making dreams come true. God alone has the ability to turn our scars into stars that light the way for others. As long as we try to be like everyone else, however, we are no better than the ugly stepsisters, who were jealous of the life they did not have. But when we step into the "shoes" (calling and destiny) God made just for us, and we say yes to His molding process, dreams really do come true.

> *Not every dream you dream is meant to come*
> *true. But the God dreams always do.*

Have you ever felt like God wanted to use you and then suddenly you lose your job, a leader rejects you, your dreams get shattered or you somehow feel displaced? Have you ever felt like you were in a waiting season or "on hold" from moving forward in your calling? Have you ever found yourself in a quiet season when no one is calling your name, no one is asking for your services and you feel isolated, even abandoned?

Perhaps you felt like you were in a cocoon, surrounded by silence, waiting to emerge from a season of transformation. You are no longer what you used to be, but you are still not ready to fly. Your past is behind you, but the vision of what you see in your future seems so far away. Think about:

- The hours of preparation needed for peak performance
- The two-a-day practices that precede great championships
- The years of study required before you can graduate

That season of waiting for your dream to manifest, but still having to mature through your process, is called *the middle*.

In the middle, you may feel like a racehorse in the starting gate, snorting and panting in anticipation, awaiting the moment you can run with passion into what you know you were born to do. So what happens when God gives you a burning vision or burden for something and then sends you through a season of dryness, darkness, solitude and barrenness?

Hold *on*, Butterfly, your change is going to come.

Don't give up. He is not finished with you yet.

Before God multiplies the vision, He will test and prepare you, the visionary, to make sure you are good and ready for takeoff. God never leaves a story in the middle of the mess. He wants to use our talents, our positions and our passions to impact the world around us. He makes all things beautiful in His timing—molding us into His image and working in us as we become reflections of His light to the world around us. And He always finishes what He starts.

BOOM!—TIME TO REFLECT

Are you ready to embrace a new life of boldness, courage and influence? Are you ready to be fueled by the fire of God and empowered to be a conduit of heaven on earth? If so, let's pray this prayer together:

Dear God,

I come boldly before Your throne, fully surrendered to Your will above my own. I am ready to give You my past, my imperfections, my fears and my failures. Take all of me. If You can use anything, Lord, use me. Echoing David's words in Psalm 51:10, create in me a clean heart and renew a right spirit within me. I want to be purified, molded and set apart for Your purposes. You are the Potter, and I am the clay. Change me, free me, pour Your Spirit through me so that I can be empowered to be a conduit of transformation in the lives of others. I want less of me and more of You, Jesus. Teach me to be more like You. Let my light so shine before others that they see You. From this day forward, I am Yours and You are mine. I am ready for whatever You send my way. I say yes! Thank You for choosing me. In Jesus' name, Amen.

5

Mindset Reset

Her setback became a setup that trained her for battle and prepared her for victory.

Fast-forward forty years, and the competitive little tomboy and overachieving basketball player had grown up and was crushing the business world as a tenacious woman with an insatiable hunger for winning. The same grit and persistence that helped me win in sports was poured into building massive sales teams and businesses that positioned me at the top of my sales and corporate game. At the top of the success ladder came accolades, awards and honors for the impressive companies we had birthed and sales records I had broken.

My income and trajectory were so substantial that my husband was able to retire from his high-stress position as COO of a telehealth company in Texas. My kids had grown into beautiful God-fearing leaders, and we seemed to be the perfect Jesus-loving, entrepreneurial family. We were traveling around the world promoting our business, which was in 25 countries.

How did the success happen? I was totally unqualified for it. With basketball, I had physical limitations—my size, height, strength and stamina. The Holy Spirit empowered me to achieve beyond my physical abilities. In the business world, I had just as many limitations. No college degree. No business pedigree to speak of. I did not have a rich dad to capitalize a start-up or cover up my mistakes.

What I brought to the table was the same tenacity and refusal to quit I had brought to the basketball court. My desire for achievement and affirmation drove me into a successful business career that demanded long hours, savvy skills and a relentless work ethic. The cutthroat corporate culture, as I soon discovered, was even more competitive and time consuming than the world of sports. And there were even more factors working against me.

Despite the stress, I pressed on with a resilient faith that with God as my agent, anything was possible. Suddenly, I was singing in front of crowds of tens of thousands of people and sharing the stage with former U.S. presidents. As a consultant in the boardrooms of Fortune 500 companies, I advised top-level executives on how to create huge company shifts.

None of this could happen in my own strength. My hard work and determination could not have carried me that far. There are many people who work much harder—and have more talent, education and experience—who never achieve close to what I was achieving. I can attribute my success only to the power of the Holy Spirit flowing through me. I surrendered my mind, my skills and my talents to God, and when He took over, amazing things took place.

In Joshua 24:13, God told the children of Israel, "I gave you a land on which you did not toil and cities you did not build; and you live in them and eat from vineyards and olive groves that you did not plant." In other words, their success was not just through their own efforts. They had supernatural provision and did not have to labor for it.

Did the Israelites have to put forth great effort to get to the Promised Land? Sure, they did. In fact, they had to overcome extreme obstacles and fear in the process. But beyond their skills came a supernatural power from God that enabled them to defeat giants that would otherwise have been impossible to overcome.

The more the children of Israel listened to God, the more He used supernatural circumstances to shift their situation. God uses the wind, rain, storms, seas and even giants to position us for greater increase. But often, He requires sacrifice as well.

Will You Say Yes?

When the enemy comes in like a flood, the Spirit of the LORD will lift up a standard against him.

Isaiah 59:19 NKJV

In the summer of 2017, I began to sense a shift taking place. On the outside, everything seemed as if we had reached the pinnacle of success, and the world would have described our lives as *winning*. Our finances were great. Our family structure was strong. Our faith seemed unshakable, our level of generosity was impressive and social media loved us and our material-rich lifestyle. I am so thankful to the Holy Spirit for the blessings He had poured upon us.

But during a trip to Africa, something began to shift in my spirit. I started to feel a deep hunger for more than all these frivolous perks that money and hard work could buy. Don't get me wrong. I loved our life and lifestyle, but deep in my core, I was not satisfied. I wanted more. The applause, accolades and awards were not satisfying the deeper longing in my heart. They never do.

As I looked around at my business success, I felt a longing, a deep and insatiable thirst for something that money cannot buy. More than anything, I wanted to be used by God to help shift our generation toward His truths. That was a desire He was putting in me. I felt the shift taking place around us, but I was not quite sure why it was suddenly hitting my emotions with such intensity.

Then, late in 2017, I was awakened at 3:00 a.m. with a new song playing in my spirit. It was a simple song, but it carried significant weight in what God was asking us to do. The lyrics of the song were:

> *Will you say yes?*
> *Will you sacrifice your life?*
> *Will you say yes?*
> *Will you raise the knife?*
> *Will you say yes?*
> *Or will you turn and walk away?*
> *Will you say yes to Me today?*

That morning, I knew God was making a request of me that would require personal and business sacrifice. What it was, I was not sure, but I knew He was asking me to shift my natural thinking to an eternal perspective. Have you ever felt as if a door were closing in front of you, one that would require you to totally rethink, recalibrate and reshape your life? That is what I was feeling in that moment. It was as if everything was changing, not only around me, but within me. What used to bring me joy now felt empty and shallow. Little did I know, God was putting the pen in my hand and about to ask me to start writing a new chapter to my story.

It was clear that God was shifting my attention from business profits and marketplace performance into making His business my highest priority with servitude as the predominant outcome. The more I meditated on the words of the song that morning, the more I realized God was asking me to dedicate the rest of my life to becoming a spokesperson for His Kingdom purposes. It was as if I was being called up to a higher purpose than mere profits or positioning. I felt a bit like Ethan Hunt in the movie *Mission Imossible*, who received a new mission assignment that he could either accept or deny.

As I sat in my office, singing the words of the new song playing in my heart, I began to dissect each word and realized that it was a calling to a life of selfless sacrifice that would be matched only by superpowers the Holy Spirit could provide. I scrolled through Bible stories in my mind that fit the narrative of the song.

> *Will you say yes?*
> *Will you sacrifice your life?*

Thoughts of Jesus suffering on the cross rolled through my head like a movie. Then I imagined Queen Esther risking her life to save the Israelite nation. I could visualize Judge Deborah leading armies into battle and Paul the apostle shackled in prison as he wrote nearly one-third of the Bible's New Testament.

> *Will you say yes?*
> *Will you raise the knife?*

More of the song played in my spirit, and I imagined Abraham raising the knife to offer his beloved son Isaac as a sacrifice to God before the ram appeared in the thickets. *What is God asking of me?* I wondered. *Am I crazy to think that He could use me to create such a monumental impact on the world? Who am I? Why me? Why now?*

> *Will you say yes?*
> *Or will you turn and walk away?*

The thought of saying no reminded me of the pressure Noah must have felt when God asked him to build an ark in the middle of a desert. People criticized him for being a "crazy" man and questioned his logic. But his obedience to the voice of God saved his family and future generations.

The more I thought about the ludicrous *yes* stories in the Bible, I realized that to say yes may mean we might have to sacrifice something monumental to follow the call of God. It could also mean giving up time with family, friends, finances and physical comforts that had become a major part of our identity and comfort zone.

I think it is fair to say that we would all like to be a superhero that saves the world from impending disaster. But saying yes does not always mean being celebrated and cheered. It often means being tortured, persecuted, ridiculed and defamed. Take it from any U.S. president. *Yes* often means having your name buried in the dirt and your family ostracized and vilified. To Jesus, it meant humiliation and crucifixion before His ultimate elevation. For the apostle Paul, it meant being falsely accused, imprisoned and tortured.

What was God asking of me? And why now? Why, after over thirty years of success in the business world, would He ask me to lay it all down and redirect my focus? I did not know what it would entail, but at three in the morning, sitting at my desk, a fierce boldness rose up in my heart as I confidently said yes to whatever He might ask.

As I was still in what I knew to be the holy presence of God, I heard God say, in His "still, small voice," *To obey is greater than sacrifice.*[1] This became my new mission: *obeying Him at any cost.* Soon I would discover that obedience was the gasoline that fueled the fire of the Holy Spirit.

God was getting ready to shake things up in my world.

Stepping into a Higher Purpose

As I looked at the state of the world, I began to see suffering everywhere. I saw the needs of hurting people around me, including the homeless in our city. Single moms who were struggling to put food on the table approached me. All around me, confusion, anger, bigotry, division and hatred were spreading through the very fabric of the institutions and organizations that once held such sacred power. Furthermore, I was aghast at what I was witnessing in the lives of women. They seemed so confused. How do they juggle home, business, work, family, gender, inequality, church and friendship?

A shift was happening, even in the Body of Christ at large. Gender roles were being questioned, and the Church was not responding with clarity. Instead, I saw conformity, acceptance and a new type of grace being taught that superseded the truth of God's Word. Soon, I became deeply frustrated watching women sacrifice their femininity and godly wisdom for the sake of inclusivity and selfish ambitions. Many even rejected their biblical values to proclaim that a human's choice is greater than God's will.

A holy anger and unrest began to rise within me. What was happening, and why now? My attention shifted away from corporate revenues and personal profits to becoming a glaring spotlight that shines on the need for a spiritual revolution. Suddenly, it was as if a blinder had been torn from my eyes and I was seeing for the first time. I saw compromise and corruption in our government, the media, front-line leaders and organized religion, and worst of all, I recognized a personal apathy, even in my own life. I felt a sudden desire to use the business acumen God had given me for over thirty years of business success to launch a new and ambitious season of marketplace ministry to this generation.

Be careful when you say yes to God because, based on my own experience, it will usually lead you to even more levels of sacrifice. On that early morning, when I heard that song in my spirit, I had no idea what was about to happen in the landscape of America and what my yes would require. I did not know that governments would become steadfast against biblical morality or that they would soon authorize the death of full-term babies in the womb.

I did not know that an uprising of women in leadership and government would begin to shape our nation's capital, and a bold and liberal movement of women's equality would try to set policies in place that were passionately set against the Word of God. Selfish ambitions and the "me" generation were being birthed, and politics would soon become louder than righteousness.

Suddenly, I could see why God had seasoned me as a communicator and negotiator for thirty years in the marketplace and why He had equipped me, as a businesswoman, with a fierce confidence and boldness to stand up as a catalyst of monumental change. I could see how the years of struggle, abuse, rejection and striving to succeed would be the very pressure needed to hone my tenacious spirit to fight back against what was clearly a spiritual battle. I felt God shifting me from the mindset of advocating for corporations into a radical boldness to fight against the diabolical agenda that was so clearly dominating the media and disrupting the spiritual DNA of our nation.

The more I saw women in politics championing marches and media campaigns that directly violated Scripture, the more I wanted to speak out for the truth of God's Word. God wants more out of me than another inspirational "rah-rah" message that created spine-tingling "goosies" on people's arms. A new revolution was being birthed in my soul, and I felt like a superhero with courage and boldness ready to be unleashed on the world.

I soon said yes to full-time marketplace ministry. Only a few months later, my husband joined me, and together, with a handful of women, we launched EMpowering Women (EMwomen.com), a nonprofit organization that focuses on helping women and girls who have suffered through some of life's greatest challenges. This soon evolved into launching EMnation.org, where we create curriculum and training for individuals, churches and organizations that further instills God's Word in the fabric of everyday society.

The day we said yes our definition of *winning* made a new shift. Now it is best defined as the victory of conquering darkness, delivering those in bondage, setting captives free, feeding the hungry, bringing healing to the sick and offering eternal transformation to those in greatest need. My deepest desire is no longer to be "in the spotlight" but to be a carrier of the light of Christ to those suffering around us.

This is why I wrote this book. God is shifting nations and waking up sleeping warriors to step into their higher purpose. I believe that is why you are reading this book. *You* are in the crosshairs of God's sight, and He is calling you to a higher place of worship. You can walk in this same power and authority once you receive and understand the fire of the Holy Spirit and how He wants to operate in and through your life. Are you ready?

BOOM!—TIME TO REFLECT

God's plan for your life is a masterpiece. And to access the abundance of all He has in store for you, you may have to step out of your comfort zone. You may have to risk everything and leap forward with tenacious faith into the life of power and authority He destined you to live. What is something you would do in life if you knew you could not fail? How would that dream, or vision, bring transformation to the people or world around you?

Pray this prayer out loud:

Dear God,

I don't want to be "normal." I want to live the supernatural life that only You can provide. I want what You want for my life, and I say yes to whatever You call me to do. Turn my ordinary talents and abilities into extraordinary opportunities to reflect Your light and Your power to the world around me. In Jesus' name I pray, Amen.

part two

FROM BROKEN TO BRAZEN

brazen (adjective):
marked by shameless
or disrespectful boldness[1]

6

Satan's Worst Nightmare

She went to bed feeling wounded and afraid. But when she woke up, the gates of hell shook and demons screamed, "Oh no! Here she comes again!"

We wake up every day to reports of bombings, mass shootings, global pandemics, shifted morality and confused systems of basic ethics. And while we have progressed as a nation in technologies and business innovation, we have digressed as a nation in spirituality, harmony and peace. The clash of good versus evil has never been stronger, and the cry for justice has never been louder. The need for superhero strength, courage and tenacity have become a necessity. But where does God find such supersonic people of faith?

The enemy abhors books likes this that will unleash God's power on the earth and resurrect marketplace giants who have fallen asleep with the lullabies of the world's agenda. Satan loves it when we play small, succumbing to weakness and growing weary in our efforts to do good. He works day and night to remind us of our past, get us to believe we are worthless and convince us we will never measure up. He hates it when a woman connects with the power of God and begins to recognize her beauty, talent and abilities will not change the world—rather, the greater One living in her has the power to move mountains.

Have you ever stopped to consider why Satan would target Eve and not Adam in the Garden of Eden? Obviously, Adam was an equal target and openly accessible as prey. Satan knew that in order to create the greatest impact against God's plan was to win over the greatest influencer on the planet. A woman.

Women are Satan's worst nightmare. That is why he tried to silence her voice in the Garden of Eden and torment her with shame, guilt, pain and suffering.

> "You will not certainly die," the serpent said to the woman. "For God knows that when you eat from it your eyes will be opened, and you will be like God, knowing good and evil." When the woman saw that the fruit of the tree was good for food and pleasing to the eye, and also desirable for gaining wisdom, she took some and ate it. She also gave some to her husband, who was with her, and he ate it.
>
> Genesis 3:4–6

Eve has been looked at, for centuries, as the weak vessel who fell to the pressures of Satan's whispers. But what if the opposite is true? What if Eve was the boldest and most courageous human on earth? What if God created her with unique abilities to influence, create and shape nations? And what if Satan was privy to that knowledge?

Think about it. This was no pushover woman. She had the gall and audacity to believe the lies that she could be as powerful as God. She saw in herself enough potential that she would rival the Creator of the universe. Satan knew he had to put a wedge between God and woman so she would fall into a weakened state and be unable to influence future generations.

Now, imagine *you* are that woman. Satan has been throwing lies, opposition and warfare against you your entire life. He knows that if he can get you to become selfishly consumed with personal power, he will destroy your greater influence. He knows that if you ever tap into your full potential, you have the capacity to totally disrupt his plans for destruction. He has worked your entire life to silence you, scare you, distract you and render you fallen, fragile and futile in winning territory over his kingdom. And he is good, *really good*, at what he does.

But God is about to flip the script on the enemy's plan for your demise. In fact, God sent the seed of His Spirit, into a woman named Mary, to redeem the loss in the Garden of Eden. Jesus, begotten of God, but born of a woman, once again proved God's intent for the female race. When a woman is filled with the Spirit, God will use her life, her womb, her talents and her dreams to shake the gates of hell.

Empowered by His Spirit

> When Elizabeth heard Mary's greeting, the baby leaped in her womb, and Elizabeth was filled with the Holy Spirit.
>
> Luke 1:41

We know Jesus was a man who became the Savior of the world. How amazing that instead of sending Jesus to the planet like Superman in a cocoon-like torpedo, God chose to put His infinitely powerful seed into the stewardship of woman. His desire to partner with woman has never ceased. God has proven time and time again that when a woman recognizes her divine mandate and is empowered by the Spirit, *anything is possible.*

Does He look at our pedigree of education or into our bank account to see how many commas we have in our investments?

Does He look for the prettiest face or the most talented people when He searches for warriors? As you read the many stories in this book, you will see that God does not look for perfect vessels. He is combing the earth in search of willing vessels. In fact, He loves using simple, foolish and often unexpected people to show forth His magnanimous glory. God does not need our talents, treasure or ego to do great things. He simply needs our yes.

A perfect example is the story of Mary, the mother of Jesus. She was a simple girl who became the catalyst of change that would shape the future of humanity. When she accepted her mission, the Holy Spirit came upon her and empowered her to birth the Savior of the world. Her relative Elizabeth, who birthed John the Baptist, also received the power of the Holy Spirit and carried out her mission in raising John to be a mighty man of God.

Mary was ridiculed. Accused of having sex out of wedlock. Elizabeth was a righteous woman but old and unable to conceive a child. In the Jewish culture, barrenness was considered to be a failure of character for a woman. In the Old Testament, Rachel said that she preferred death to childlessness (see Genesis 30:1). These women did not have a perfect story. In fact, they faced tremendous adversity, which is why they needed the power of the Holy Spirit to fulfill the mission God had for their lives.

In the same way, you do not have to have a perfect story to create significant change in the lives of others. You might be a quiet teacher who is chosen by God to create life transformation in a room full of future world leaders. You may be a struggling business owner who creates a solution that fills a void in the marketplace. You could be a mom, feeling insignificant while changing diapers, not knowing you are raising a child who will change the world.

What you need is the Holy Spirit living inside of you, giving you superpowers that transcend your natural talents and capabilities. When a woman, empowered by the Holy Spirit, fully submits to the greater call of God upon her life, she becomes a lethal weapon in the hands of God and a penetrating force against the kingdom of darkness. Her life takes on new purpose. No longer paralyzed by past traumas or failures, she stands unshakable, immovable and truly unstoppable.

Never underestimate the power you have and the influence God has given you.

Water into Wine

Having spent most of my life in traditional churches, I have heard just about every story in the Bible. Usually, when preachers talk about Jesus, they do so from the lens of a male disciple or apostle. But when I think about Jesus, I like to consider the viewpoint of Mary. How did this remarkable man, who was both God and human, grow to have such tenacious courage? Who taught Him how to think outside the box, silence His critics, stand strong in the midst of adversity and break the mold of the status quo?

Many believe that Joseph died early in the silent years of Jesus' life. While we do not have firm documentation of that opinion, we do know that Scripture speaks very little of Joseph after Jesus is found reading Scripture in the temple at the age of twelve. From that day on, we only hear about Mary's role in influencing Jesus' adult life.

Jesus was raised to be a world shaker and a history maker. He was prepared to rival kingdoms and live with the "It's Not Over Till I Win" perspective. When Jesus turned thirty years of age, it was time for Him to go public with His ministry. Being the influencer she was, Mary had done her part, and she knew it was time to cut the apron strings and let Him set the world on fire.

At first, Jesus resisted Mary's suggestion to perform a miracle in public by turning the water into wine. Maybe it was the look in her eyes that only a mother can give that convinced Jesus to rethink His decision. I can see her walking up to Jesus and saying, "Houston, we have a problem. Son, the wine has run out, and You know how Your cousins get when the vat runs dry. Now's the time to take Your superpower out for a spin, and let's take this party to the next level!"

But Jesus acted like He was a bit perturbed by her request. Again, in my world of creative imagination, I can see the thirty-year-old Jesus saying, "Really, Mom? Haven't we talked about this? It's not time, and when it is, I will know it." But Scripture does not tell us what happened next. All we know is Mary's look must have been piercing enough that Jesus quickly followed His mother's suggestion and lit up that party like the Fourth of July.

God uses women as influencers to make shifts happen. Mary gave Jesus the push He needed to come out of the shadows and reveal His greatness. In John 2:1–5, we see Mary's influence over Jesus on full display.

> On the third day a wedding took place at Cana in Galilee. Jesus' mother was there, and Jesus and his disciples had also been invited to the wedding. When the wine was gone, Jesus' mother said to him, "They have no more wine."
>
> "Woman, why do you involve me?" Jesus replied. "My hour has not yet come."
>
> His mother said to the servants, "Do whatever he tells you."

What happened next would shape history. Jesus listened to the influence of His mother, performed His first public miracle and launched into full-time marketplace ministry. While the miracle of Him turning water into wine is significant, so is the fact that God used a woman to influence the launch of this powerful revolutionary into His higher purpose.

Mary, though often portrayed as a follower of Christ, was first an influencer, mentor, life coach, strategist and mom. Jesus, like other Jewish boys, had been mentored by His father to work in a specific trade in the marketplace. Joseph was a *tekton* (a Greek word usually translated as "carpenter" in the Bible)[1] or what we know today as a craftsman, builder or stonemason.[2] No doubt, God chose Joseph to father Jesus on earth for a season and teach Him skills that would give Him relevancy in the business world and knowledge about negotiations, trade and religion. After Jesus turned twelve, we stop hearing about Joseph but continue to see the impact of Mary in His life until ultimately, she gives the little eaglet the nudge He needs to soar like an eagle and fly.

> This miracle at Cana in Galilee was Jesus' first public demonstration of his heaven-sent power. And his disciples believed that he really was the Messiah.
> After the wedding he left for Capernaum for a few days with his mother, brothers, and disciples.
>
> John 2:11–12 TLB

What happened after Jesus turned the water into wine? He began to do all kinds of signs and wonders throughout Cana, and many believed in Him and became disciples. Who was with Him? His mother. She was not the only one, but was the first one mentioned. She prompted Him to perform a miracle. Jesus resisted; she persisted, and her influence changed the world.

Fierce and Fabulous

Women are powerful. Since creation, women have been noted as influencers with the innate ability to uphold and equally tear down kingdoms. The impact one women can have on this earth is monumental, and Satan has been working 24/7 to destroy her influence on earth. But he is failing—big-time.

Look at these statistics:

- Today, women control over $20 trillion in worldwide spending.[3]

control more than 60 percent of all personal
n the United States.[4]

purchase over 50 percent of traditional male prod-
:luding automobiles, home improvement products
and consumer electronics.[5]

- Approximately 40 percent of U.S. working women now
outearn their husbands.[6]

- Women make 90 percent of household health care
decisions.[7]

- "Over the next decade, women will control two-thirds of
all consumer wealth in the United States and be the ben-
eficiaries of the largest transference of wealth in our country's history. Estimates range from $12 to $40 trillion."[8]

- Women earned 61.6 percent of all associate degrees, 56.7
percent of all bachelor degrees, 59.9 percent of all master's
degrees and 51.6 percent of all doctorate degrees in 2013.[9]

- In 2019, about 76.8 percent of mothers whose youngest
child was 6 to 17 years old participated in the workforce
by having at least one job.[10]

Clearly, women and their influence in the marketplace is spreading throughout the world.

Women today are expected to multitask, serve, lead, influence,
conquer and overcome their weaknesses and emotions while man-
aging schedules, shuffling kids to practice, cooking dinner and pre-
venting the breakout of World War III in their home. God was in a
good mood and knew what the world needed the day He decided
to create woman. He knew she would be a fierce and fabulous force
of change in the world. He would use her life struggles and pressure to create a resilient, creative, emotional and limitless warrior.

Now is the time for women to become living conduits of God's
power on earth. As business mavericks, entrepreneurs, moms, poli-
ticians, lawyers, doctors, executives, Uber drivers, social workers,

entertainers and friends, we are powerful beyond words. We can no longer be apathetic to the growing animosity of darkness, perversion and division that permeates our nation. We cannot sit back in our corner offices of padded perfection or quiet closets of peaceful contemplation and let the world around us continue to decay. Clearly, for things to change, we must change, and God has given us the power, timing and authority to do so.

While confusion and moral decay seem to be screaming in the ears of our children, there is a growing force of God chasers who are hungry for a move of God and ready to rise up as catalysts of change in the marketplace and world. As a female leader, I feel deeply called to awaken my inner warrior and stand up for God's truth as a woman of faith—liberated and empowered, not by politics or policies, but by the power of the Holy Spirit and the truth of God's Word. You are powerful beyond words, and despite the many plates you will spin, you have been equipped by God to birth revolutions and revolutionaries.

We are waking up a generation of sleeping warriors, both male and female, young and old, who are ready, willing and able to be the voice of spiritual truth that this generation so desperately needs. That is why my husband and I were quick to say yes to God's voice and step away from our pursuit of profits and become passionately devoted to pursuing His higher purposes. We know God is shifting kingdoms to bring healing to the nations of the earth. He is about to bring new order to the seven pillars of society, including the areas of faith, family, education, government, media, entertainment and business. The question is, Will you allow Him to give you a superhero cape, a sword and a shield to be His agent of change this generation so desperately needs?

No matter what you have been facing or how difficult life has become, let God awaken your inner warrior and then say yes to whatever He asks you to do. Let Him teach you to discern His voice so that you will become a fierce, bold and righteous leader in your workplace and at home. Get ready to know the Holy Spirit of

God intimately, and continually invite Him to be your Counselor, Advocate and Guide. Then boldly, you will take dominion over any principality that would endeavor to hold you back.

If you have ever felt the painful emotions of rejection, abandonment or fear, hang on tight because God is not finished with you yet. "He who began a good work in you" *is faithful to finish what He started* (Philippians 1:6). The best pages of your story are still unwritten, and God is about to turn your mess into a monumental message of victory.

As you continue reading through the pages of this book, stop and ask God to awaken you to His masterful plan for your life. You may think your life is insignificant, but those kids of yours could be the world changers and history makers God needs to shift this generation. You might think nobody knows or even cares how hard you work to stay afloat, but rest assured, God is watching, and He is preparing you for something remarkable.

BOOM!—TIME TO REFLECT

No doubt, God was in a good mood the day He decided to create woman. She is designed with inherent abilities to influence the world around her. Stop for a moment and think about your own life. Where do you believe you have the greatest influence today? Who is impacted by the choices you make? How can you use your influence to ignite God's purposes and bring change to the world around you?

Pray this prayer out loud:

God, I want to be a vessel You work through. Use my life, my voice, my skills and even my mistakes to glorify You. I recognize that being a woman is a special gift You have given me, and I want to know how to use my feminity to become

Your hands and feet to the world around me. Teach me to be powerful yet humble, resilient yet kind. Let my gentleness speak louder than my desire to be right or my need to lead. I want to reflect the woman You see in me and use my influence to change the lives of those I meet. Teach me, Holy Spirit, I pray. In Jesus' name, Amen.

7

Fearless and Courageous

She was unstoppable, not because she was without fear, but because she had the courage to overcome it.

As a businesswoman, I have experienced, firsthand, the endless struggle of climbing the corporate ladder, searching for fulfillment in my titles, salaries, awards and even in the success of my marriage and my children. Unfortunately, I have also felt the suffering and stress that the pursuit of "more" can yield. Enough never seems to be enough when we are living under the patterns of a world immersed in greed, selfish ambition, high performance and human power. After reaching the pinnacle of success in my career, I still found myself starving for significance and feeling a lack of fulfillment. What I discovered in my process of liberation and enlightenment has led me to a life of peace and profits, one that has awakened my spirit, soul and body. It has helped me realize that every battle, every mountain, every storm that has come my way was never sent to destroy me but to prepare me for the next season of victory that was about to emerge. I have found that greater levels of success demand a deeper commitment to humility and a surrender to the God of the impossible.

Not Your Everyday Entrepreneur

Look at these words of Jesus, which should be our words today:

> "The Spirit of the LORD is upon Me, because He has anointed Me to preach the gospel to the poor; He has sent Me to heal the brokenhearted, to proclaim liberty to the captives and recovery of sight to the blind, to set at liberty those who are bruised and oppressed."
>
> Luke 4:18 NKJV

Jesus did not hide behind fancy titles, costly walls of institutions, political offices or temples. Instead, He unleashed God's power in the marketplace, on the streets and in the homes of ordinary people ready for extraordinary change. Jesus' life was the most exceptional example of how to franchise a message of hope, help and healing that would build a lasting legacy for eternity. Instead of representing the brick-and-mortar temples made by man, Jesus taught us how to be fluid like water, teaching His followers how to seep into the crevices of society and immerse the marketplace with the Good News.

An *entrepreneur* is "a person who organizes and operates a business, *taking on greater than normal risks* in order to do so."[1] Jesus was an entrepreneur before He was a rabbi. He was a stonemason in the marketplace before He was known as a miracle worker. He was an out-of-the-box thinker, a culture-shaker, a mindset disrupter. He was God in a human body, and yet He operated, like you and me, as a visionary with a cause. Some saw Jesus as a rebel, while others saw Him as a revolutionary. *Rebels merely try to overturn the past while revolutionaries risk all to change the future.* To walk with Jesus as a woman disciple was risky business, and those who did so had the courage and willingness to sacrifice all for the sake of His message.

We search for purpose in our jobs, talents or professions, but we were not born to merely build empires and incomes. The search for success will never fulfill your longing for greater significance. That proverbial hole in your heart can only be filled when you engage your higher purpose. Today's push for gender equality seems, to many, to be the answer to heal the pain of suffering. But the truth is that equality, though noble and good, is never going to heal our need for greater spirituality. Our equality is an inalienable right given to us by God. With that understanding, a woman can go into the marketplace with boldness—not with a chip on her shoulder, but with the power of the Holy Spirit permeating every aspect of her being.

That is why, as leaders, we must recognize the divine calling behind our jobs, companies, homes and possessions. Our jobs are a mission field of people we can reach every day. Our schools are full of hurting hearts we can impact. Our communities are filled with individuals suffering from hopelessness and living with physical pain. And our homes are more than status symbols; they are platforms, positioning us in neighborhoods that need light, love and liberty. Whether your primary sphere of influence is in a schoolhouse, courthouse, the White House, a boardroom or within your own house as a stay-at-home mom, God wants to partner with you and empower you to be His eyes, ears, voice, hands, feet and heart to a lost and hurting generation that is crying out for attention.

But the question remains, Are we using the talents and positions God has given us to further His reach, or are we merely looking for what pleases us? The temptation to focus on selfish ambitions stifles God's purposes on earth and limits our fullest potential. When we become selfishly consumed with our house, our bills, our bodies, our suffering and our needs, we lose sight of lost and hurting neighbors, co-workers and people around us who are crying out for help. But when we step out of our ivory white towers and allow God's Spirit to flow through us, we can indeed become catalysts of the change we want to see in the world.

In the previous chapter, we looked at Jesus' mother, Mary—another revolutionary thinker. Most Bible teachers depict her as a meek and unassuming girl, chosen by God to birth the Savior. But what they fail to show is that same young girl grew into a highly influential leader, empowered by the Holy Spirit to persuade the Son of God when to launch His public ministry. When she attended the wedding feast, she recognized and seized the moment when the wine had run dry. She put her influence and courage into action and asked her miracle-working Son to turn water into wine. When opportunity arises, women like Mary are often first to create the most revolutionary solutions that change history. Women are problem solvers and great critical thinkers when empowered by the Holy Spirit.

Today, your most significant acts of goodwill and spiritual enlightenment will not come from an elaborate platform, fancy office, eloquent speech, expensive building or even institutions of learning. It will be birthed through ordinary people like you who allow the Holy Spirit of God to use them to unleash His message and presence in their everyday lives and throughout the world.

Risk Takers in the Bible

According to a report released by American Express, as of 2017, "there are an estimated 11.6 million women-owned businesses in the United States that employ nearly 9 million people and generate more than $1.7 trillion in revenues." [2] Over the past twenty years, the number of women-owned businesses has grown 114 percent compared to the overall national growth rate of 44 percent for all businesses.[3] Today, some of our greatest and most used inventions came from women who saw a need in the marketplace and created a solution to fill the void. The first car heater, fire escape, life raft, computer algorithm, refrigerator, ice cream maker and dishwasher,[4] as well as SPANX,[5] were all created with women's ingenuity and ability to see solutions. Those innovations and more have literally changed our lives forever.

What Satan recognized in the Garden of Eden is becoming common knowledge today. *Women are risk takers*, even though most would say they are not. From Eve to the women of the New Testament and even to the women rising in power today, God has always had a masterful plan to empower women to be victorious in life as risk-taking entrepreneurs.

Old Testament Risk Takers

Eve, the first woman in creation, was the initial risk taker of all time. While bold and adventurous, she was also a perfect example of the destruction that happens when selfish ambition gets in the way of our God-given purpose. She had everything humanly possible on earth, and yet she was willing to risk her life for the selfish ambition of "more." Women, though often the weaker vessels in Scripture, were still born with a resilient courage to do whatever is necessary to provide for their family.

Deborah was a judge and a courageous leader who was willing to risk her life to lead an army into victory. She could see an outcome of great power and financial gain and was willing to do what her counterparts were unwilling to do. Esther used her beauty and courage to save her people from annihilation. In story after story in the Bible, we see the fearlessness of women who used their cry for justice to create progress. God was very strategic to put these powerful women and their superhero stories at the forefront of Scripture.

Kingdom Investors

In Luke 8, we read about three bold and financially stable women who were among the greatest financial contributors of Jesus and the disciples.

Not long afterwards he began a tour of the cities and villages of
Galilee to announce the coming of the Kingdom of God, and took
his twelve disciples with him. Some women went along, from whom
he had cast out demons or whom he had healed; among them were
Mary Magdalene (Jesus had cast out seven demons from her),
Joanna, Chuza's wife (Chuza was King Herod's business manager
and was in charge of his palace and domestic affairs), Susanna,
and many others who were contributing from their private means
to the support of Jesus and his disciples.

Luke 8:1–3 TLB

Mary Magdalene had seven demons when she first met Jesus.
She was a hot mess for sure! After Jesus healed her, however, Mary
and seven other ladies became the primary financial supporters of
Jesus' ministry. Joanna, the second woman in this Scripture, was
Chuza's wife. Chuza handled all of the finances for King Herod, a
baby-murdering king who wanted to destroy any boy child who could
possibly be the Messiah. God positioned Joanna with great courage
so that she could use her influence and financial wealth to fund Jesus'
ministry, the very ministry Herod so passionately wanted to destroy.

Do not let the fact that you are a woman with a past minimize
your potential for influence. Jesus was no respecter of persons, nor
did He prioritize gender. He looked for obedience.

Freed from Sin and Shame

The Scriptures tell the story of a woman who was caught in the
act of adultery. She was living a life of sin and shame. A group of
religious leaders threw her body to the ground at Jesus' feet, but
look what He did not say. He did not say, "It's great to meet you.
I want to invite you to come to church with Me on Sunday. We
have great worship music and a super cool pastor who will give
you a sermon of hope." Instead, He took immediate authority
over darkness and gave us a "how-to" clinic in setting captives

free right where they are in the marketplace. Jesus was a conduit of heaven on earth, and that is exactly what we are to be, as well.

What happened after the woman was set free? She went back to her hometown and told everyone she knew about what happened. To do that, she had to be set free of her shame. It did not bother her to go tell everyone that she was guilty of adultery. So many people today want to hide their sin. She did not. As shameful as her story may have seemed, her freedom gave her the courage to tell others how Jesus turned her torment into a testimony of mercy. She took on the same spirit of Christ.

Hope to the Hopeless

"If the Son sets you free, you will be free indeed."

John 8:36

One day a woman came to me for prayer. "Staci, I don't understand how you have such an undaunted boldness," she began. "I look at you and see a fiery courage, and I want that so much. But honestly, it's just not in me!"

As I listened further, I began to connect the dots on her story, learning she had been molested as a child and her parents did not believe her when she told them at the age of eight. She had lived most of her life imprisoned by shame, anger, abandonment and fear. She was afraid to speak up, thinking no one would listen to her and angry that God had allowed the suffering in the first place. She had layered the pain of her childhood with the additional shame of sin, sexual immorality, abortions and excessive drinking.

Her life had become a snowball of emotions and bad decisions—all as the result of something she had no control over in her past. The enemy was holding her hostage, bound with the memories and emotions that were linked to her past. He was blinding her from seeing her full potential by influencing her to focus on her past pain and suffering. Her current life was beautiful, but she could not forget her past. Her sense of shame and pain had muzzled her power. Her choice to add sin to her story only served to compound her sorrows, giving her a sense of separation from God.

Now, 25 years after the molestation, here she was sitting in front of me, ready to implode emotionally as she replayed the event and the rejection of her parents over and over and over in her mind. Her therapist had done everything possible for her. She even took numerous prescription medications to help her cope with the pain. But this woman needed more than money could buy, and her place of need was deeper than a medication could reach. She did not need a creative breathing technique or a mental strategy to cope with her past. She needed freedom.

Broken, battered and spiritually blinded in my office that day, she was not a threat to the kingdom of darkness because her voice had been muted and her courage stripped. I looked her in the eyes and paused before speaking. Under my breath I said, "Satan, you've messed with the wrong woman. She is about to be activated for Kingdom purposes. You should have never allowed her to get into my office. Your time is up, and *it's not over till she wins!*"

I prayed with her that day for sudden freedom and immediate release of all shame, pain, fear, anger and every foul and toxic emotion brought on by the enemy. As a bold and confident carrier of the Holy Spirit, I took authority over those spirits and watched as this precious woman was set free in Jesus' name. Her countenance changed, and her body language shifted into a more powerful posture of expectancy. She went from sullen and afraid to having a desire to see God use her story to make a difference in the lives of others. What therapy and medication could not do was all changed in one moment with the King.

This was why Jesus came to earth. He saw the suffering of humanity and the separation they had from the Father. Whether He was in the temple courts, the mainstream marketplace or a synagogue of worship, He was a living, breathing, walking, talking move of God.

Jesus was the one who set Mary Magdalene free of seven demons, and He is the same one who set the woman in my office free of her own demons. Jesus is still setting people free. But He is setting them free for a purpose: so that people might know Him and the power of His resurrection and to make His name great in all the earth.

BOOM!—TIME TO REFLECT

You are powerful beyond words. Your life has the potential to be a nuclear weapon against the forces of darkness. But first you must surrender to the greater plan of God. Like all the heroic women in the Bible, you have seeds of greatness packed within your life, simple as it may seem, that are waiting to be watered and nurtured into something marvelous. Your womb of creativity is God's gift to this world. What you make of it is your gift back to God. It is up to you to use the power and authority He has given you to shape the universe around you. What fears, habits or regrets are you still living with that you need to surrender to God so He can turn your ordinary life into an extraordinary conduit of His courage, power and authority?

Pray this prayer aloud:

God,

I see now that You had an intentional plan for my life as a woman. You were in a good mood when You made me. I was not a mistake; I am a marvelous, wonderful, powerful temple of Your Spirit. I refuse to let the enemy convince me that I am weak, forgotten, broken or abused any longer. I receive Your Spirit of strength, wisdom and courage. Thank You, God, for making me uniquely me! I dedicate my past, my present and my future into Your hands so that You can turn me into a fearless and courageous woman of truth. I ask this in Jesus' name, Amen.

8

Claiming Your Inheritance

Tiaras and castles do not make a queen. But her legacy of generosity and truth speak of her royalty.

Recently my husband, Larry, and I endured a long and arduous process at an auto dealership in order to purchase a new vehicle. At times it was frustrating to have to wait patiently for the "sales process" to take its course. And by the time the negotiations were over, the various associates had worn me down. Then suddenly, I heard a small whisper.

Why are you so focused on the price of the vehicle when I've sent you here to connect with the people in your pathway? I've placed you in these offices to be My light in the marketplace. Use this time to connect with the people I sent your way.

In that moment, I had a choice to make. I could make my reason for being in those sales offices merely about making a purchase, or I could listen to the voice of the Holy Spirit and elevate my consciousness to become the hands and feet of Christ in that very moment. For a moment, I was so consumed with *my* needs that I almost missed being a part of God's handiwork in the lives of others.

As I stopped and took a big breath, I tapped into the "mind of Christ" (1 Corinthians 2:16 KJV) and shifted into my God-given role as a messenger of hope. The business manager walked in and took her seat. I took time to connect with her and find out more about her time at that dealership. Lovingly I told her about our ministry for women and could sense a connection being made.

"You know, I care more about people than I do vehicles," I said out of the blue. "Is there anything I can pray with you about today?"

She laid her pen down and looked me straight in the eye. "As a matter of fact, yes, there is." She proceeded to share with me details about events that were taking place in her life. After Larry and I prayed with her, tears of gratitude filled her eyes.

The result? Not only did I get a remarkable deal, but I was also able to pray for the salesman, the inspection specialist and the general manager before we left the building. Each of them was facing different life circumstances that they would call significant and life changing.

As we were leaving, a delivery specialist came to our vehicle and said, "Hey, I felt led to come back to the dealership after I made it home to see if you had been taken care of. I was with my kids but could not get away from the feeling that I needed to come back and see you."

I looked at her and said, "Can I pray for you? That is what I do and why I believe God allowed me to purchase at this location."

"Yes, I know," she said. "I heard about you praying for people here."

"Is there something I can pray with you about?" I asked.

She proceeded to tell me her story and the immediate needs in her life. Then we prayed together. She cried and said she felt a shift taking place in her heart.

Now imagine how things might have turned out differently if I had only focused on the vehicle and missed the opportunity of being God's light in the lives of the people in the process.

God wants to use our lives in more ways than we can imagine. He is not looking to put everyone on a stage with a microphone, but He *is* looking to put us in offices, grocery stores, libraries, schools, dealerships and everyday locations where we can bring hope, help and healing to others.

God wants to equip us to be His agents of change throughout the marketplace so He can unleash His spiritual authority and boldness through us. We are carriers of God's light and love, and we are empowered to take the fire of His Spirit to the world around us. Now is the time for a marketplace revolution of miracles to begin, and it starts when we say, *Yes, God! Use me. Send me. Flow through me, and let my life, my job and my talents bring hope, help and healing to the world around me.*

Get What Is Yours

"We feel that we should be given property along with our father's brothers."

Numbers 27:4 TLB

Numbers 27 tells the story of five daughters who were mourning the unfortunate death of their father. Without sons to carry on his legacy, the father's inheritance, family name and generational impact were about to be cut off forever. The law stated that only sons could receive a father's inheritance, leaving daughters in a state of inequality and dependency on their brothers or husbands upon a father's death. Rather than ranting and raving, his five unmarried daughters gathered together and recognized that if they remained broken and silent, their father's legacy would end, and his inheritance would go unclaimed.

A sudden boldness took over their hearts as they approached the entrance of the Tabernacle. They called on Moses, Eleazar (the priest), all the tribal leaders and anyone else nearby. With great resolve and wisdom, the daughters made a formal request to recognize women as rightful heirs to their father's kingdom. "Our father died in the wilderness," they explained (v. 3). He was not one of Korah's followers, who revolted against the Lord; he had died a natural death. Why should the name of their father disappear just because he had no male heirs? "We feel that we should be given property along with our father's brothers" (v. 4 TLB).

> So Moses brought their case before the Lord.
> And the Lord replied to Moses, "The daughters of Zelophehad are correct. Give them land along with their uncles; give them the property that would have been given to their father if he had lived. Moreover, this is a general law among you, that if a man dies and has no sons, then his inheritance shall be passed on to his daughters. And if he has no daughter, it shall belong to his brothers. And if he has no brother, then it shall go to his uncles. But if he has no uncles, then it shall go to the nearest relative."
>
> Numbers 27:5–11 TLB

Shut the front door! Have you ever read that Scripture? I had never seen that passage before until my friend sent it to me during one of my writing sessions on this book. These women were world-shakers, history makers and law changers. They shifted women's rights and positioned daughters as rightful heirs to Kingdom legacy.

These ladies might have been broken due to the circumstances of their past. They were not going to sit back, however, and let old laws and outdated thinking keep them from their inheritance. Instead, they used their story to shift the narrative. Their brazen boldness changed the law, causing Moses and the leaders to rewrite policies on behalf of the entire nation of Israel. And not just Moses, but they moved the heart of God, who made sure that the laws that needed to be changed were corrected.

These women did not put on false masculinity or trade in their natural femininity in order to gain the attention of the powers that be. Instead, they simply used wisdom, logic and the favor of God. This is a huge lesson for women today. The enemy would love to silence you and steal your inheritance. He would also love for you to think your battle is against men in high places. He wants you to believe that you need to go into "beast mode" and muscle up like a man, strap on a suit or drop the neckline in order to get what is rightfully yours. But Scripture after Scripture shows us that a woman's femininity, discernment, wisdom and courage are enough to shift kingdoms and save nations.

Satan knows the power of the female voice and has been waging war against women like you for eternity. He will stop at nothing to get you to believe the lies that your income, financial status, positional rank, public opinion, past abuse or suffering are due to the men in power around you. He wants you to see people as your enemy and your struggle as a human battle. He does not want you to see that he is the great manipulator, the accuser, the ultimate adversary, the father of lies and the puppet master behind all human suffering.

> For we are not fighting against people made of flesh and blood, but against persons without bodies—the evil rulers of the unseen world, those mighty satanic beings and great evil princes of darkness who rule this world; and against huge numbers of wicked spirits in the spirit world.
>
> Ephesians 6:12 TLB

Satan would love for you to spend all your effort fighting against people made of "flesh and blood," waging war in human battles and creating division with the very people God has ordained you to influence. His goal is to keep you away from the inheritance that has your name on it in heaven because you are a child of the King. When you recognize the real enemy of your destiny is not the people around you, the Holy Spirit will give you the ideas and strategic plans you need to gain territory. This is what it means to be fueled by fire or empowered by the Holy Spirit. Take the lead from these five women: *Get what is yours*, and let the Holy Spirit give you the wisdom on how to do it.

Marketplace Missionaries

"Go into *all the world* and preach the gospel to all creation."

Mark 16:15, emphasis added

When my daughter, Alexia, turned sixteen, she was overjoyed to get her first job. I remember the pride she had going to work at Chick-fil-A that first day, wearing the company uniform and hat like a badge of honor. But soon, after smelling like cooked chicken and standing on her feet all day, she realized that a job means hard work and sacrifice, people can be grumpy and selfish, and life could be perfect if only human emotions were not involved.

After that first week, awakened to the fact that some had no regard for her "winning attitude," my daughter came home ready to quit. "Why do I have to do this job when it has nothing to do with my real dream of being a worship leader?" she asked.

What she did not understand was that her job was God's gift to her to touch the world and worship Him through servitude and sacrifice. People create pressures, unrealistic expectations and frustrations to our ideal dream of peace and the pursuit of happiness. People cause our egos to roar and our emotions to cry "foul." And yet, the very people who surround us at work and in life are our mission field; we have been sent to reach, love and impact them with the Good News of Christ. Standing behind that counter, Alexia was expressing worship to Him without ever singing a song.

"Baby," I told her, "those people who come into your Chick-fil-A are your mission field, and that cash register you stand behind is your pulpit. Worship God by letting your light shine to everyone who walks up to your cash register. Be light. Be love. Be Jesus in the marketplace. And then, when you prove faithful to reflect Him in the little things, God can make you ruler over much."[1]

In your lifetime, you will spend approximately ninety thousand hours in the workplace. In those precious hours of your life, no one is exempt from the challenges, stress and frustration that come with the struggle to find the winning edge, grind for power or provide for the family. Today, more than ever, we need God in the workplace, in the marketplace, in schools and in our homes. We need men and women who live fully awakened to what is happening around them and how the enemy is at play. We need Warrior Queens to become conduits of the Holy Spirit for a people starving for leadership worth following.

Perhaps you can understand those feelings of frustration with your job, employer or workplace. Ask yourself, *Why am I here? Why has God enabled me to be placed here, right now, in this season? Whom has He positioned me in this place to reach?* If we merely live to fulfill our selfish motives of personal gain and notoriety, we are living for ego and will ultimately find it an empty path to suffering, broken relationships and defeat. When we recognize our true purpose and potential, however, we will see that every job, every negotiation, each challenge and every adversity we face is an opportunity to reflect God's love, power and peace to the world around us.

A Church without Walls

We spend forty to fifty hours a week at our jobs. We spend even more time shopping in the marketplace, going to school, attending sporting events and frequenting entertainment venues. We live busy lives. Now, compare the time we spend in the marketplace to the average *one* hour a week we spend in a place of worship, where someone reads Scripture to us or delivers a message designed to grow our faith.

What many people know as "church" is merely a large group of people sitting comfortably in a large auditorium-like setting, week after week, listening to the same speaker talk about stories in the Bible. As creative and inspiring as the messages might be, they do not scare the enemy. He could not care less if you sit in an auditorium or in a pew once a week and get inspired. He loves it when God's people have the mistaken belief that "attending church" is enough. But what scares the hell out of the demons of darkness is when the Body of Christ, inspired by those Bible stories and messages of truth, takes the power of God into the world around them.

It is clear to see why Jesus chose to break out of the walls of the traditional church or synagogue structure and establish a new model of ministry in the marketplace. He knew the best way to reach hurting people would not be through the brick-and-mortar establishments with a hierarchy made by man, but through the spiritual awakening of ordinary leaders, like you and me, who would be willing to go share their faith with others. That is why Jesus sent the Holy Spirit to live *in* us and work through us.

"Do you not know that your bodies are temples of the Holy Spirit, who is in you, whom you have received from God?" (1 Corinthians 6:19). In that Scripture, Paul is not saying your local church is the temple of God, and if you want to encounter Him, you must go there on Sunday. No, *you* are the temple of God, and His Spirit is in *you*. That changes everything. That means that you can encounter God daily, right in your office cubicle, car or house. And better still, you can take Jesus to the workplace, schools and everywhere you go. This is the big shift we need in today's communities. Now is the time to awaken the Body of Christ and teach them to get out of their seats and into the streets.

The term *going to church* has confused a lot of people. You do not *go* to church. You *are* the Church. You are the living, breathing Body of Christ. God wants *you* to lay hands on the sick. He wants *you* to bring freedom to those bound to addiction and oppression. As a part of the Body of Christ, we gather in communities (many call them churches) to worship together, celebrate testimonies, study the Word of God and equip people to take His presence into the world. But do not be misled: The Church is not found in a brick-and-mortar establishment. The Church is the people of God, and they are the living stones of His temple.

Do not just go to church—*be the Church*.

Jesus poured out His Spirit on *all flesh*, not just a chosen few good speakers. His power is available for every Christian. That means *you*. Fully embracing the power of the Holy Spirit in your life will turn you from a passive bystander into a radical mouthpiece for God. He wants to raise a massive army of believers to be deployed into the world and *be* the Church.

Be the light. Be Jesus in the marketplace. Be a revolutionary. Birth revival and start a fire of evangelism that cannot be contained. This is the heartbeat of God.

BOOM!—TIME TO REFLECT

Have you done all you can do to be a conduit of light in the marketplace around you? Are you focused on scaling your numbers or achieving your goals more than serving your co-workers? Do you reflect God and His love for humanity, or are you a walking ego searching for personal recognition, affirmation and significance through your efforts? When was the last time you prayed for someone in the marketplace or boldly led someone to the Lord? Think of a time when you know God used you to be a source of hope for someone else. How did it make you feel?

Pray this prayer out loud:

God,

Please forgive me for being selfish. Forgive me for being so consumed with my own life that I failed to be the conduit of light You have called me to be for others. Teach me to be more like You, Jesus. Holy Spirit, give me the courage and boldness to reach out to others and pray for them, love them, and care for them. May I show Your loving mercy toward them in their time of need. Let my life become a vessel You flow through. Whether it is to my family, to my co-workers or in my community, let my life be a living example of Your faithfulness, and let my actions speak louder than words. I pray this in the mighty name of Jesus, Amen.

9

Anointed for Battle

She was unstoppable, not only because she had the courage to overcome her fear, but because she had enough courage to silence her enemies.

I grew up in the day and age when we suntanned our bodies by smearing on layers of baby oil or even worse, Crisco. I can remember hoping that lying outside in a Walmart swimming pool, lathered with oil, would somehow turn my pale-white skin into a luscious golden glow. Unfortunately, all too often, I ended up looking more like a lobster or the sunburned girl on the Coppertone commercials. On the other hand, looking back on those careless days of ignorance in the sun gives me a clear picture of what it means to be anointed from head to toe.

What Is God's Anointing?

Samuel took the horn of oil and anointed him in the presence of his brothers, and from that day on the Spirit of the Lord came powerfully upon David.

1 Samuel 16:13

The word *anoint* is a verb that means: 1) "to smear or rub with oil or an oily substance"; 2a) "to apply oil to as part of a religious ceremony"; 2b) "to choose by or as if by divine election."[1] When God anoints you, He pours His Spirit out upon you and fills you with His power to overcome. When you are anointed by God, your mind gets lathered with His Word and the Holy Spirit becomes the loudest voice in your head. There is no such thing as a powerless Christian if that person has truly been filled with the Holy Spirit.

Here is another reason why God's anointing is so important: Satan's highest ambition is to convince you it is okay to think like the world, act like the world and have emotional anxiety like the world. If he wins that battle, he owns your mind and distracts you from being the weapon of truth and power that God has destined you to be. If the enemy can persuade you to become so emotionally toxic that you disrespect your authorities at work, divide your family, gossip at church or subtly allow character flaws to creep into your environment, he can and will destroy your peace, your prosperity and your purpose to make God known throughout the earth.

The ancient origin of the word *anointing* came from the practice of shepherds in the field whose primary business activity was tending sheep, multiplying their flock and selling or trading them for profit or consumption. Much like a modern-day business that creates and markets goods and services, sheep were a huge commodity and so was their meat, wool and skin. If a shepherd's herd of sheep was threatened, so was his job and his income, which is why protecting the herd was of great importance.

Back then, the greatest threat to sheep losing their lives was not lions or bears or other predators. Instead, the number-one killer of sheep was the lice and insects that would creep into their ears and kill the sheep from the inside out. To combat this issue, shepherds anointed the sheep's heads with oil, a lot of oil. They poured enough oil over the sheep's head that it would make the wool slippery and impossible for insects to get near their ears. That is also how the practice of anointing became symbolic of blessing, protection and empowerment. As time passed, the oil signified the Holy Spirit of God poured out on the head of individual people, consecrating or setting them apart for specific roles of leadership such as a king, prophet, builder, etc. (see Psalm 133:2). In essence, they became the sheep of God, hearing His voice and deflecting the voice of the enemy.

David, the little shepherd boy who became famous for killing the giant, Goliath, was more than a kid tending sheep in a field. He was a young entrepreneur, learning to rule and reign by overseeing the expanding inventory of his father's sheep business. The world saw him as the runt of the litter. He was the least among his brothers. The "other" child. Surely there were days he heard those voices and wondered if he could really measure up.

David's primary job as a shepherd was that of a security guard. He had to make sure that shoplifters (aka lions and bears) would not steal from his father's production line of sheep. David had to resist the thoughts of fear. You can imagine this young boy having to sit with the sheep in the middle of the night, listening for bears, lions and other threats on the prowl at night. Satan knows that if he can attack your thoughts and emotions, he can kill, steal and destroy you from the inside out.[2]

Perhaps the lies of the enemy have tried to make you feel less than significant as well. But when others saw merely a shepherd boy in David, God saw a king in the making. There were many times when the Holy Spirit "came upon" David and empowered him to win battles. We have an advantage David did not have. While the Holy Spirit came upon him for short periods of time to empower him, the Holy Spirit lives in us all the time so that we live in constant power.

When God looks at you, He does not see weakness, failure or fractures. He sees a woman on purpose, reading a book in order to take action and become a vessel of honor. David did not have to rant and rave about his strength or importance to others. In fact, he may not have even realized that off in another land, God was preparing the way for his destiny. David did not have to picket or protest for equality in order to be heard. He was not busy creating marketing ploys to self-promote his greatness. Instead, in due season, God shifted kingdoms so that David's divine mandate could be fulfilled.

Mental strength in those early days of opposition are what prepared him to be a mighty warrior and king later in his life. God used the voices of opposition to strengthen David's resolve. Soon, he found himself taking lunch to his older brothers on the front line of battle. What he saw as he approached the battlefield, no doubt, came as a shock. As he ran up to the front lines of the battle, he noticed the "elite" and highly trained soldiers of Israel had all retreated in fear because of the constant verbal insults of the Philistine giant, Goliath. But when young David saw the verbal exchanges, he was not moved because his mind was set on the power of his God. His mind was already anointed to be king. His mind was already under the covering or protection of the Holy Spirit.

David sized up the situation with Goliath, and while the other Israelites saw the challenge as too big a risk, the entrepreneurial risk-taker in David rose to the challenge. He asked, "What's in it for the man who kills that Philistine and gets rid of this ugly blot on Israel's honor? Who does he think he is, anyway, this uncircumcised Philistine, taunting the armies of God-Alive?" (1 Samuel 17:26 MSG).

Let's revisit the definition of entrepreneur from chapter 7: one who "organizes and operates a business, taking on greater than normal risks in order to do so."[3] David saw a golden opportunity for financial increase and advancement. Instead of being insecure and succumbing to voices of fear, he had full confidence in the power of his God. He walked up to the negotiation field, ready to close the deal and gain the plunder. Perhaps he thought, *I've killed lions and bears who were faster and more agile than this big and clumsy giant. It's not over till I win! God, let's do this.*

And so, David used his weapon of choice—a slingshot. The battleground was his stage, and the gawking soldiers of Israel were his mission field. That day, he sent a prophetic message to the masses that his God was supreme in all things. David fulfilled his human purpose in that very moment: *to know God and the power of His resurrection and to make Him known throughout the earth.*

The entire Bible is full of examples of men, boys, women and girls who yielded to a higher voice and greater calling than their inner critic. They learned to embrace risk, live with courage and conquer the battlefield of the mind. This is only possible with the power of the Holy Spirit.

Silencing Your Inner Critics

Now it is God who makes both us and you stand firm in Christ. He anointed us, set his seal of ownership on us, and put his Spirit in our hearts as a deposit, guaranteeing what is to come.

2 Corinthians 1:21–22

As women who want to stretch beyond success and into lives of lasting significance, we will need the protection and power of the Holy Spirit to stand up against the temptations and forces of evil in this generation. Jesus assured us that we will face opposition, and it will be risky to stand up for what you believe. Haters will hate.

In a world where anyone and everyone can "comment" on your life and choose to "like" or frown upon your pictures and posts, opposition can open the door to even louder self-talk. *I'm not good enough. I'm too old. They will never accept me. I can't seem to lose this weight. I hate these wrinkles. Why did God give me such big hips? I hate my boss. I just can't seem to focus. I'm tired, and I just can't take this anymore.*

These are just a few of the statements your inner critic might have whispered in your ear this week. These are the voices of the enemy, and they do not stop at words of deprecation. They dive deeper and target your deepest emotions. Fear, anxiety, stress, anger, bitterness, greed, envy, selfish ambition and lust are the outcomes of the voices that play like a broken record over and over and over in our minds. Satan loves it when we listen to these spirits because he knows we will self-sabotage if we ever allow them to sink into our minds.

Let's imagine you have a big promotion on the table and right before you go in for your interview, a co-worker walks into your office, looks you up and down and says, "You're not wearing that, are you? That outfit makes you look fat and your eyes look tired!" Chances are, you would either be irate or emotionally disturbed that she would have the audacity to speak to you like that right before your big interview. You may even want to usher her out of your office with a swift kick in the booty. But as ridiculous as that sounds, that is exactly what we allow to happen when we entertain the negative voices and inner critics that play over and over in our head.

Self-doubt, insecurities, fear, anger, resentment, greed, pride, lust, bitterness, hatred, jealousy, regret, grief and sorrow are just a few of the negative emotions that manifest due to the battlefield in our minds. They are weapons of warfare the enemy uses to destroy our influence. When we let toxic thoughts take root in our lives, they produce toxic emotions that create a stench to others. Instead of being magnetic, we repel the very people we are called to reach. When we learn to renew our minds with the power of God's Word, however, we take captive the very thoughts the enemy tries to use against us.

In her book *Think, Learn, Succeed*, Caroline Leaf wrote:

A growing body of evidence shows how our thought lives have incredible power over our intellectual, emotional, cognitive, and physical well-being. Our thoughts can either limit us to what we believe we can do or free us to develop abilities well beyond our expectations or the expectations of others. When we choose a mindset that extends our abilities rather than limits them, we will experience greater intellectual satisfaction, emotional control, and mental and physical health.[4]

Toxic thoughts that produce toxic emotions turn a beautiful woman into a trash collector.[5] She starts to take on the smell of offense and bitterness instead of walking into a room with humility and grace. Instead of brightening the room when she enters, it lights up when she leaves. Instead of being a sweet-smelling fragrance to the Father, she is full of sour attitudes that create a stench to His nostrils. This is Satan's plan against woman, and he sends destructive voices and thoughts to keep her from becoming the carrier of light and influence God has destined her to be.

> For though we walk in the flesh, we do not war according to the flesh. For the weapons of our warfare are not carnal but mighty in God for pulling down strongholds, casting down arguments and every high thing that exalts itself against the knowledge of God, bringing every thought into captivity to the obedience of Christ.
>
> 2 Corinthians 10:3–5 NKJV

When it comes to winning, the greatest adversary you will face will not be the people, places or things that appear in broad daylight around you. Instead, it will be the deceptive voices and spirits lurking in the crevices of your mind, waiting to exploit your darkest fears and most toxic emotions. When toxic thoughts or emotions are allowed to build up or "stack" in your life, they begin to take up space that could be used for greater purposes.

"Stacking" is a principle of allowing emotions to pile up on top of one another until a sense of anxiety, chaos or self-sabotage is reached.[6] By focusing on the circumstances, people or pressures around you, a feeling of being overwhelmed can take place, causing the human mind to lose practical consciousness. Stacking old emotions is like a teenage boy throwing his dirty socks in the corner till finally the stench is overwhelming. When we stack emotions, instead of "sifting" them, we pile up toxic time bombs till eventually one little thing sets off an explosion of monumental proportions. In other words, you go cray-cray and start acting like a bat out of hell. Eventually, too much stacking can lead to a nervous breakdown, anxiety attacks, eating disorders, sickness and disease, broken relationships, suicidal depression or even self-harm. This is a tactic of the enemy, who wants you to keep your eyes and ears focused on the pain of your past, the offenses of others, circumstances that are out of your control and the ugly attitudes of those around you. By paralyzing you with toxic emotions, he renders you unfit for Kingdom purposes.

But God has offered this wisdom as a way of escape from stacking or focusing on the circumstances of your life. The key is focus. What are you "fixed" upon? What do you think about most on a daily basis? What has captured your greatest attention?

"You will keep in perfect peace all who trust in you, all whose thoughts are fixed on you!" (Isaiah 26:3 NLT).

The challenges we face on a daily basis are 10 percent circumstantial and 90 percent how you deal with those circumstances spiritually and emotionally.[7] Unfortunately, most people spend a relatively small percentage of their day in any type of spiritual or emotional training. Instead of strengthening their spiritual muscles and practicing the art of scriptural meditation, breathing or intentional focus on God's Word, they spend hours in the gym or on social media trying to win the favor of the people or peers around them. But to win in business, family and life while maintaining peace in the process, you *must* learn to fight from a different perspective.

That is why the Holy Spirit was sent to live in you and has anointed you with power to win over the threats and tactics of the enemy. You are about to awaken to the irreplaceable value of the Holy Spirit's role in your life and how to protect your mind, heart and body with the armor of God. By the end of this book, you will be educated, equipped and empowered with everything you need to take dominion in the marketplace and get back everything the enemy has ever stolen from you or your family (see Joel 2:25).

BOOM!—TIME TO REFLECT

Your mind is a powerful source of creativity, innovation and wisdom when surrendered to the control of the Father. When left to its own devices, however, your mind can become a playground for the enemy to plant weeds of destruction and chaos. Do you have thoughts, negative feelings, self-doubt, anger, resentment, feelings of abandonment or other dark emotions that wage war on your mind?

If so, say this prayer out loud:

Heavenly Father,

I come to You now, in Jesus' name, with confidence and boldness, to ask that You silence the negative voices in my mind. I take authority over my thoughts and emotions, even now, and I command all spirits of darkness to leave my mind, in Jesus' name. Holy Spirit, fill me with Your presence and flood my thoughts with Your thoughts. Cleanse me now from all unrighteousness, and show me if there is anything in my life or home that might be opening the door to the enemy's work against my destiny. I ask this now, in the mighty name of Jesus, Amen.

part three

ARMED AND DANGEROUS

armor (noun):
defensive covering for the body
especially : covering (as of metal)
used in combat[1]

10

Buckle Up Tight, Warrior Queen

The Belt of Truth

And suddenly, she stood up out of the ashes, brushed off her armor and yelled, "Not today, Devil. You are messing with the wrong queen, and it's not over till I win!"

I remember the days when the WWJD (What Would Jesus Do?) bracelets were a hot commodity. Youth groups everywhere were handing out the bracelets to help students make better decisions. Eventually, the trend caught on in mainstream sales, and people of all ages were wearing the bracelets as a fashion statement. When I met Larry, I was passionately focused on full-time ministry and using my voice to record Christian music that helped people have a deeper relationship with Christ. I also hosted a weekly Bible study group and taught a program I wrote called "Pledge for Purity."

When I saw Larry for the first time at the gym, he was a body-builder and former football player for Texas A&M. He was in a season of hard-core training for the Mr. Oklahoma Bodybuilding Championship. At six foot five inches tall with 8 percent body fat, Larry was a massive, physically perfect hunk of a man. He spent two to three hours a day chiseling his physique.

But while Larry was physically perfect, he was spiritually shallow. After we met, I invited him to a Bible study I hosted each week. As you can imagine, when he walked into that Bible study, the girls shouted privately, *Hallelujah, God has sent me the man of my dreams!* The first night he attended, he surrendered his life to God and was filled with the Holy Spirit. He began a spiritual journey of radical transformation as each week he embraced becoming more balanced—spirit, soul and body.

As he continued to grow and learn more about becoming a man of God, he wore a WWJD bracelet every day to remind him of his highest priority. Soon, it would be time for his bodybuilding competition, where he was slated as "the one to beat." At the gym one day, he said to me, "I am having second thoughts about participating in the Mr. Oklahoma championship."

I had felt it coming, knowing he was drawing closer and closer to God, but his peers were shocked. "Why on earth would you have second thoughts when you're picked to win?" they asked.

Larry replied, ever so humbly, "There was a time when winning would have been the greatest thing on my mind. I have spent years preparing to win this competition, and I know that I might be letting some people down. But every day when I work out, I look at this WWJD bracelet, and I think to myself, *Would Jesus get up on a stage, in a Speedo, and pridefully pose in front of people to show off His chiseled body?* I can't imagine a humble king wanting to put a spotlight on His flesh with the hopes of winning an earthly prize."

He went on to explain why he pulled out of the competition and stepped away from the world of bodybuilding altogether so he could enroll in Victory Bible Institute in Tulsa, Oklahoma. "I've spent most of my life working on my body and mind, and it's time I balance things out by giving greater attention to my spirit." And BOOM!—he broke out of mediocre thinking and into the "mind of Christ" (1 Corinthians 2:16 KJV).

Suddenly Larry, who was once fueled by competition and selfish ambition, became fueled by the fire of God burning out his fleshly desires and filling him with the mindset of Christ. Then, and only then, did God put a spotlight on Larry for my eyes to see. One year later, I fell in love—not with a beautiful man, but with a warrior of God who could rule and reign the Kingdom and family God would entrust us with. He had won my heart not because of his physique but because of his passion for Christ.

For most of his life, Larry had believed the lie that his value was in his size, strength and athletic ability. But once he cinched the "belt of truth" firmly around his waist, according to Ephesians 6:14, he began to hear God's voice, want God's best and live God's way. And you, too, "having girded your waist with truth" (v. 14 NKJV)—by stepping off your pedestal of pride and surrendering your mind, body and *spirit* to the One who makes lasting love, peace and prosperity even possible—are saying, *Not my will, but Thine be done, Lord Jesus!*

Put On Your Armor

> Put on the full armor of God, so that you can take your stand against the devil's schemes. For our struggle is not against flesh and blood, but against the rulers, against the authorities, against the powers of this dark world and against the spiritual forces of evil in the heavenly realms.
>
> Ephesians 6:11–12

As a mentor to young Timothy, Paul was making two important points in Ephesians 6. The first is a position of defense when he speaks of being fully covered by the armor of God so that he can stand firm against the enemy's strategies that are targeted at killing, stealing and destroying internal peace. The second part of this Scripture teaches us how to also fight back with weapons of spiritual warfare.

Armor is a defense strategy to help protect your body and most vital organs against attack. Spiritual armor is God's defense mechanism to protect your mind, will and emotions from the deceptive voices of the enemy. If you feel yourself succumbing to thoughts of depression, anger, confusion, anxiety or fear, chances are, you have dropped a piece of your armor and you need to stop and reposition yourself for victory. When you are suited up in the full armor of God, however, you can stand boldly in a room, postured with confidence, peace and authority.

When Paul so eloquently describes our spiritual armor, he was inviting us to recognize that the secret to his success in winning over darkness was not a coincidence but a critical part of his spiritual strategy. Having been a great persecutor of Christians before his spiritual conversion, Paul was very aware of the tactics of the enemy against God's people. His wisdom to young Timothy was based on experience and the same source that gave Jesus the power to overcome the enemy in His greatest times of temptation and even persecution.

Paul went on to say,

> Therefore put on the full armor of God, so that when the day of evil comes, you may be able to stand your ground, and after you have done everything, to stand. Stand firm then, with the *belt of truth* buckled around your waist.
>
> vv. 13–14, emphasis added

The belt, also known as the *cingulum* or *balteus*, of a Roman soldier in Paul's day, was not a Gucci fashion statement like some people wear today. Instead, it was a thick, unbreakable piece of leather that wrapped around the waist with heavy metal and draped down a soldier's front to protect the loin or reproductive area. The belt also played a crucial role in holding a sword.[1] Without the sword, there would be no offensive battle plan to advance against the enemy.

Satan's attack against Christians in the marketplace is to remove the belt of truth from the workplace, government offices and our educational system. Without truth, the enemy can deceive and manipulate people into believing his lies, which always lead to physical and emotional imprisonment. His plan is 100 percent focused on deception. He uses illusions, lies, twisted morality and temptations of the flesh to compel us to think that God's Word is outdated, irrelevant or too judgmental for today's culture.

One of the ways he does this is to convince Christians that you cannot speak up for the truth of God's Word because it might offend someone. On social media, for example, if you talk about modesty, abstinence or a biblical view of marriage, others will say, "You're being judgmental. You should be more like Jesus, who loved all people just as they are." But the truth is, while Jesus loved all people in their sin, He also loved them too much to leave them there. That is why He spoke boldly about truth *and* love, and we must do the same. The day we stop declaring truth is the day the enemy sweeps in and blinds a generation to his lies. This is how prayer was removed from schools, the Ten Commandments from public locations and biblical morality from the fabric of our society.

Recognize Your Place

In the game of chess, the queen is the most powerful game piece on the board. Unlike other chess pieces, the queen is unlimited and unrestricted, making her power undeniable. She can move onto any unobstructed square and in any direction—forward, backward or diagonally. She can take over any position on which the opposing piece stands. Her influence on the chessboard is unmatched, which is why it is so important to give her not only freedom to reign but also fortified protection from enemy forces.

Queens of great kingdoms do not sit in high positions hoping to hide behind ivory white towers of palatial privilege. They do not shield themselves from the decisions needed to be made in order to protect their kingdom. They are instead keenly aware of the wars that threaten their throne and its people. As queens today, we must stay engaged in the spiritual battle of prayer that overtakes enemy forces that would try to prevail against our families, jobs, communities and nation.

There is a war raging all around us. It is real. It is a fight for territory and an assault against the soul of humankind. It is an epic battle of good versus evil. And no one, no matter how young or old, is isolated from the impact of its carnage. This battle can be seen in the divisive spirits of politics, media and entertainment, and its aftermath can be felt by the hatred, immorality, rebellion and selfishness that has permeated our society. Being aware of the real battle at hand should be the priority of every woman and every queen on God's chessboard. It is our responsibility to recognize the influence and power we possess to shift the minds and hearts of those around us so they come into full submission to God's higher purposes.

Choose Your Battles Wisely

"Then you will know the truth, and the truth will set you free."

John 8:32

As a black belt in mixed martial arts and a former basketball player, I remember the ritual of gearing up for a match. My uniform was a very important part of my identity and a declaration of which team I was playing for. In martial arts, wearing my black belt was a symbol of rank, position, practice and preparation. It spoke of my dedication and commitment to the sport and told my opponent I was not a rookie fighter. In basketball, everything from the tape around my ankles to the shoes on my feet and the jersey on my back put me in the mental frame of mind to go out and gain victory for the team I represented.

Prior to the day of competition, I spent hours upon hours preparing for my opponent. I not only made it my practice to be a good offensive player, but I also studied the defensive strategies of the opposing team so I could outwit, outlast and outplay them on the mat or court. I wanted to know their tactics before ever getting in the game of competition.

Likewise, knowing who and what you are fighting against in life is critical in winning everyday battles at home, with your children, in your marriage and in the marketplace.

Calculate the risk of each move, conversation, emotional outburst or response you might make before you ever make them. Getting engaged in a war of words or emotions can leave collateral damage that you have to clean up years after the battle is over. Remember, the enemy of lies wants to trip you up with a spirit of bitterness or offense in order to throw you off your A game of peace and paralyze your progress.

The enemy wants to penetrate your family, business, marriage and life. This is why putting on the full armor of God is vital to protecting your life and the peace God has called you to walk in. Spiritual warfare means recognizing that people are not your enemy. Your husband is not the bad guy. Your kids are not your opponents. Your co-worker or boss is not the real adversary. They are mere pawns in the enemy's plan to render you emotionally unfit for Kingdom purpose.

If you underestimate who your real opponent is, you will fight people instead of fighting the principalities who are really at play. If you fail to recognize the spiritual battle you are facing, you will argue with loved ones, shout words of self-defense and cry out against the people who you are called to influence. In business, we may try to win contracts with cunning words or deceptive antics, but if we want to gain *Kingdom* territory, we must learn to fight in the Spirit.

Let's look at that defense strategy more clearly and how it relates to our effectiveness in business, family and life.

Protect Your Legacy

One translation reads, "Stand firm therefore, having girded your loins with truth."[2] This Scripture talks about protecting the loins—the breeding ground for reproduction and duplication. When we wear the belt of truth, we are applying a protective covering over our loins or all things that equate to multiplication, reproduction and legacy.

If, on the other hand, you let down your guard and allow the belt of truth to become unbuckled, you will no longer be representing God's Kingdom or His best for your life. In business, when truth is evaded, corporate values succumb to mistrust, greed and deception. No one wants to work in an environment of half-truths or manipulation. To protect your work environment from division and discord, make sure the belt of truth is in place to protect the legacy you most want to leave.

In our families, truth leads to legacy. When a family stands for biblical truth, it flourishes. When lies and deception enter our homes, however, children rebel, marriages are violated, emotions grow toxic, and suddenly, no matter how many words you try to speak to fix the problem, the lack of truth breeds division. Satan loves it when business leaders exaggerate numbers or let their egos inflate their reality. Why? Because it unbuckles the belt of truth around their loins and leads them to long-term impotency.

Think about how tempting it is to let "little white lies" into your relationships or workplace. It is so easy to embellish the truth or create a story that is blown out of proportion when sitting with clients at dinner. Then ask yourself if somehow you have allowed mistruths, shady manipulation or ego-centered motives to invade your life.

Satan is a master deceiver. He whispers in your ear, telling you that a little white lie will not hurt you. In fact, he wants you to believe that lying is the fastest way to achievement and success. He knows that if you start with one mistruth, you will have to tell more lies to cover up the first one, until finally your belt is gone, your loins are exposed and your impotency as a leader is ensured.

Satan's goal is to twist you up in a world of deception, lies and confusion until you are convinced that you are bound by the mistakes of your past. But the truth of God's Word offers you freedom and deliverance from the deception of the enemy. That is why Jesus came to show us a better way. He is the key to your freedom, and He gives you back the belt of truth so that you can wage spiritual warfare on the enemy.

Jesus said, "I am the way and the truth and the life. No one comes to the Father except through me" (John 14:6). The best way to know and reflect Jesus is to know and reflect the *truth* of God's Word and follow the example that He gave us. This is also the greatest way to protect your legacy and your overall ability to duplicate *life* to others.

Perhaps you have been misguided by the enemy to believe that your talent, your face, your body or your job are what will lead you to the greatest areas of joy and peace in life. When you put on the belt of truth by studying what God's Word has to say about your future, you will see that God relationships and God positions could be waiting on the other side of the lies the enemy has been telling you.

BOOM!—TIME TO REFLECT

There is no such thing as a little white lie and no such thing as "almost" true. God is calling us to refuse the manipulative tactics of the enemy and resist his mental games by choosing to be women of truth—not just in the big things, but in all things. Do you have any areas of half-truth you need to surrender to God in order to close the door to the enemy? Can you think of a time when you knew there were forces fighting against you, your family or your business? In moments like that, what is your greatest move as a queen on God's chessboard?

God,

I know You know my secret sins. You know when I lie down and when I get up. Nothing is hidden from You. Forgive me, Father, for the many times that I have lied, cheated or used my words and actions to manipulate others. Purify my heart, renew my mind and restore me back to perfect union with Your Spirit. I resist the deceiver and the source of all lies, and I surrender my life to You, O God. I am clean. I am clean. In You, I am clean. In Jesus' name, Amen.

11

Guard Your Heart above All

The Breastplate of Righteousness

As the smoke cleared, everyone could see the reflection of her breast-plate shining through the remnants of her garments.

When my children were toddlers, a massive fire broke out in our home. Alexia was barely able to sit up, and Payton was two years old. On that particular day, we were having a birthday party for a friend and 25 people were expected to show up at any moment. I needed something from the grocery store, so I took Payton with me, leaving Alexia sitting on the floor with her daddy. Larry was smoking brisket and chicken, putting his man card on full display for his friends, who loved the mastery of his smoker skills.

When I returned from the grocery store, I noticed black billowing smoke coming from what looked like our subdivision. As I got closer, it appeared to be coming from our street. When I turned the corner, I saw the neighbors and Larry in a panic trying to douse our roof with water hoses. Once they realized the four-alarm fire was too big to contain, they started pouring water on their own roofs until the fire trucks appeared. Every firefighter in Prosper, Texas, showed up for the big event.

To my amazement, two weeks prior to that date, I had awakened in the middle of the night with a dream that our home was on fire. In my dream, an air filter fan we had placed in a room had caught on fire. I rushed the kids and puppy out of the house and secured all my scrapbooks and irreplaceable keepsakes. The dream was so real that when I woke up, I checked on the kids, then went downstairs to move my precious collectibles to a more secure place. You can imagine the shock and awe when I turned the corner to see our home on fire two weeks after my dream. A strange and eerie peace flooded my body as if I had already been prepared for what was about to happen.

The fire burned for more than seven hours. Firefighters put their lives on the line to save our home while neighbors pulled out their lawn chairs and beer to watch our home burn from their driveways. It was quite the spectacle, and despite the drama, I knew that somehow God would use these circumstances for our good.

The kids and dog were safe, but the fire chief refused to allow us to enter the home until they identified the source of the fire. It seemed like forever as we waited anxiously for the chief to give us the word that we could go make one trip inside to grab our most irreplaceable belongings. Our guests arrived for the party and prayed with us as our home was up in flames.

Finally, the fire chief said, "We've isolated the origin of the fire. It is in the eaves of your roof, so you can make only one trip in to get what you think you can't replace."

When our friends heard his statement, they ran into the house like a land rush to grab anything they could. I knew exactly where to go because I had placed my most precious possessions securely in a large box in the cabinet of my front office. So I ran in, grabbed it and ran out. I could barely see five inches in front of my face due to the amount of smoke in the home.

Once outside the home, I saw friends rushing in and out of the front door with pictures, clothes and anything they could grab. Then one man came leaping out of a first-story window with my underwear drawer. I about fell over, thinking to myself, *Oh dear. Let 'em burn, let 'em burn!*

Such a crazy sense of adrenaline rushed through our veins.

Then, miraculously, a woman we had never seen or met before walked straight up to Larry and handed him a twelve-inch box containing his championship football rings, his grandpa's WWII treasures and special keepsakes money cannot buy. Larry had hidden this treasure trove on his side of the bed—no one else knew it existed. Larry stood in total shock that this woman knew exactly where to look in her single sweep of the home. No one knew who she was or where she came from, and we never saw her again.

After the mad rush, first responders restricted us from going in again and instead, forced us to stand in the street and watch as they tried to salvage our home.

A news reporter arrived on the scene and approached me. "Ma'am, is this your home?" he asked.

I smiled. "Yes, it is."

"You seem to have a lot of peace for someone whose home is on fire."

Immediately, God's Word poured out of my lips. "Well, I know that 'all things'—even the seemingly worst things—'work together for good to them that love God' and are 'called according to his purpose,'" I said, quoting Romans 8:28 (KJV). "I don't know how or when, but God will use this for good."

As he walked away, a song flooded my heart in a matter of minutes. Here is what I wrote:

> Thanks for the joy that You've given to me
> Thanks for Your love unconditionally
> Thanks for peace in the midst of the storm

Lord, I thank You
Yes, I thank You
You've been faithful, faithful to me

Lord, You're faithful
Your mercies I see
And when I look back on my life, the message is clear

Lord, You're faithful
And I thank You
Thank You

The Word of God was our life filter, and knowing its truth protected our hearts in times of trouble. We knew we could rest on the promises of God to work this crazy situation out for our good. And He did. Boy, did He ever! That fire became a financial blessing to our family, and the insurance settlement allowed us to rebuild it in such a way that we could host prayer meetings, choir rehearsals, women's Bible studies, Holy Spirit classes and more for a new church we were helping birth in the city. God used that fire to start a ripple effect of miracles that still impact our community today.

Don't Forget Your Breastplate

> Therefore put on the full armor of God, so that when the day of evil comes, you may be able to stand your ground, and after you have done everything, to stand. Stand firm then, with the belt of truth buckled around your waist, with the *breastplate of righteousness* in place.
>
> Ephesians 6:13–14, emphasis added

For a Roman soldier in biblical times, the breastplate (*cuirass*) was a part of his critical defense strategy because it provided protection

128

to his thorax or chest area. The thorax is the area between the neck and abdomen that contains vital organs such as the heart and lungs.[1] Without a solid breastplate, a soldier leaves himself open for unexpected attacks that could become instantly fatal. When Paul encouraged God's people to put on the breastplate of righteousness, he was keenly aware of how the enemy targets the major decision centers of our lives.

Satan is an evil and deceptive liar. Scripture says that he masquerades or dresses up as an angel of light. He loves to send chaos, heartache and confusion into our lives through people, pressures and circumstances. He wants us to doubt God, and he especially targets women because of the influence they wield. Much like he did the heart of Eve in the Garden of Eden, his lies are directly aimed at manipulating our emotions and twisting truth to make us believe his lies are more trustworthy than God's Word. He wants us to accept the lie that God is to blame for our suffering. He wants women to believe that God does not understand a woman's needs or that He is somehow out of touch with today's pressures. This lie has led to women believing they have the right to decide whether a baby should live or die.

"It's my body. It's my life. It's a woman's choice." Satan wants us to believe that our thoughts are higher than God's thoughts and our ways are higher than God's ways. He wants women to believe that pregnancy is not something God is involved in but merely a natural outcome of sex. The enemy wants us to believe that conception is natural, not miraculous. Thus the conversation about a woman being god of her own body. How could God be involved in an unplanned pregnancy that occurs during a woman's drunken stupor or due to a man's raging hormones? How could God possibly be big enough to have purpose for a baby's life conceived unplanned or without human purpose?

Satan has twisted and confused an entire generation of women to believe that morality is not based on the truth of God's Word, but on the circumstances the woman is faced with. In other words,

God's Word is not absolute and needs to be governed by the will of mankind. This has led our society to believe that we get to choose our gender, we get to choose our morality, we get to choose our baby's fate, and we get to act as demigods of our lives. This is the definition of what it means to live without a breastplate of righteousness.

Wearing a breastplate of righteousness means you have positioned God's Word as a priority in your decision-making process. It means you have placed God's standards as supreme authority over your mind, your will and your emotions. Scripture is over your heart like a protective covering and filter for every decision you make. When you allow a biblical worldview to determine the heartbeat of your decisions, you will make choices that protect your spiritual core.

When our house was on fire, instead of a spirit of fear, Scriptures poured out of my lips and praise permeated my heart— proof positive that my breastplate of righteousness was secure. Instead of being worried or emotionally devastated, I could sit in perfect peace, knowing that nothing the enemy could throw my way would be more powerful than God's ability to turn it around for my good. As we covered earlier, the enemy's arrows are not physical weapons but spiritual forces that are sent to kill, steal and destroy your joy, hope, unity, prosperity and life.[2] The weapons sent to take you out and penetrate your heart could be arrows of offense, hatred, unforgiveness, selfishness, greed, immorality and more. The enemy knows if he can penetrate your heart, he can control your life. Once the heart stops, life is over.

The Heart Attacked

Heart disease is the number-one killer in the world today.[3] Spiritual heart disease is the number-one weapon of the enemy against your eternal purpose. Guarding your heart is essential to the life and impact of a marketplace warrior today. If the enemy can steal your heart, he knows he can win your soul. By influencing your heart away from the things of God, Satan knows he can put a spiritual blindfold on your eyes that distorts your vision and your ability to discern right from wrong. This is why you must, above all, "guard your heart" (Proverbs 4:23).

Of equal importance is protecting the heart of your family. This means protecting their values, morals, unity and unconditional love. When mistrust, anger, selfishness or division take place in the heart of a family, the enemy knows he has penetrated the breastplate and is targeting vital organs that lead to fatality. That is why it is so important to know that you are not fighting people, but you are warring against principalities that use people to create division.

What are the *issues* that consume your mind, will and emotions daily? Where is the real attack on your emotions, family, business or marriage? The breastplate of righteousness will enable you to have a life that is impenetrable against the spiritual attacks and will help you see clearly the tactics of the enemy.

My child, pay attention to what I say. Listen carefully to my words. Don't lose sight of them. Let them penetrate deep into your heart, for they bring life to those who find them, and healing to their whole body. *Guard your heart above all else*, for it determines the course of your life.

Proverbs 4:20–23 NLT, emphasis added

This Scripture is encouraging us to embrace God's Word, meditate upon the Scriptures and take them deep into our heart as if they were an invisible force field or shield of protection. The more we know the Word of God, the more we will reflect it. Jesus used the Word of God to be a shield against the temptations of the enemy in the desert when He said, "It is written . . ."[4] Over and over, He declared the Word of God as the standard of truth and morality for His human existence. The devil tried to twist the truth and fabricate

131

reality, but not only did Jesus know the Word—He *was* the Word made flesh. His standard of righteousness was unshakable because His life was a perfect reflection of what it means to stand in right relationship before God. This test of the enemy was the final exam before Jesus was elevated into public ministry. Standing the test of righteousness will no doubt be a major test in our own lives, as well.

In my own life, I know when my breastplate is down because the enemy creeps in with lies of depression, failure and sorrow. He loves to target a woman's heart with rejection, failure, isolation, loneliness, abandonment and a search for approval. He loves to remove her from the protection of family, friends, community and spiritual mentoring so that he can become the loudest voice in her ear. Ladies, don't get caught in this trap. Stay connected to the very people and places that are designed to protect your heart and keep your mind and emotions centered on God's Word.

Though we are powerful and full of potential, every warrior is a child underneath her armor. If your heart is broken or heavy, you know the feeling of fighting battles without your breastplate of righteousness. If you have ever fallen prey to sexual immorality or temptations of the flesh, you are keenly aware of how the enemy sneaks around like a roaring lion, searching for prey.

There have been days when I have found myself so broken, alone and weary that I would curl up in the fetal position and pray for Jesus to return. Those moments were always the result of allowing toxic emotions, deceptive spirits, sharp-edged opinions or depressive thoughts to penetrate my soul. I remember one day specifically, when I felt like all of my life's efforts in helping women were in vain. I listened to voices that dug like daggers into my heart. *You are not good enough. You are spinning your wheels*, they said. *No one really loves you, and no one really cares that you want to change the world. You are a wannabe leader, and if you died today, the world would go on and never miss a beat.*

Thirty minutes before that state of depression, I had been scrolling through Instagram looking at the perfect life and ministry of every other Warrior Queen on the planet. The more I compared myself to their successes, the more I felt depressed. As I watched woman after woman posting the magnificent perfection of their lives, the more I felt the illumination of my failures and shortcomings. Ugh. What a depressive state to be in. I lay in bed crying like a baby and spiraling into an abyss of darkness.

Suddenly, I was at the end of my rope and I determined in my mind to quit and return to corporate America, where I could gain the respect I thought I really deserved. I was engulfed in the master of lies and I had taken his bait—hook, line and sinker.

Then my husband came into the room and rescued me by saying, "Get up! This is not you, and the more you listen to those voices, the more likely you are to quit on the very women God has called you to reach."

"But I don't want to do this anymore," I said. "I feel so alone. I'm not anointed to save souls. I'm best when I'm making money. Then I can put in big offerings for other people to win the lost." I know, sounds pathetic, right?

"Really? You really believe that is truth speaking to you right now?" Larry replied, empowered by the Holy Spirit. "Are you really going to let those voices win and take you out? Is that all you've got?" He knows my competitive spirit and how to get me riled up. But that day, even my competitive heartbeat was dead.

I rolled my eyes and put a pillow over my face. "*Yes* . . . I quit!"

He walked out the door and left me to lie in my pitiful vomit of apathetic misery.

Then he came back and opened the door. "Fine, you quit. Go ahead and abandon the women and girls who are out there crying for rescue. Turn your back on the very ones you have been sent to save. I will go after them myself. I will run this women's organization with or without you."

After what seemed like an eternity of silence, he asked, "Are you finished? Are you really giving up?"

"No," I replied, like a dog with its tail between its legs. "I don't quit. I'm getting up."

He made me take a shower with the sound of the worship song "Way Maker" by Sinach playing in the background and then sat me down to speak Scripture into my heart. Soon, my head was clear, and my heart was beating with truth. I could feel the breastplate of righteousness repositioned over my heart and the wounds of the battle slowly healing themselves through the power of God's Word.

How is your heart today? Perhaps you know that same fetal position of wallowing in misery due to the circumstances around you. Maybe you do not have a husband who can stage an intervention by walking into your room and yanking you out of your emotional abyss. But I believe God allowed me to have that moment so I could write this message to you today. These words are sent for you to get up, shake off your death garments, take a spiritual shower of worship and reposition your breastplate of righteousness.

The Proof of Righteousness

> Therefore, if anyone is in Christ, the new creation has come: The old has gone, the new is here!
>
> 2 Corinthians 5:17

Righteousness means living in a way that honors God. When, however, we fail to live according to Scripture, we choose to live without our breastplate of righteousness and we expose our heart, our mind and our emotions to the enemy. A life without righteousness is like a banana without a peel. It is a life exposed to the enemy and ready to be devoured.

When you are in good standing with God, however, you can hold Him to be faithful to His Word. He cannot lie. He is a good, good Father. That is the peace that comes with the breastplate of righteousness. It is not something you achieve, but it is something given to you by the Holy Spirit to help protect your heart in battle. It is a covenant reward for those who live their lives in the righteousness of God in Christ.

When the apostle Paul encouraged us to put on the breastplate of righteousness, he was not suggesting we must live in perfection. Instead, he was offering *protection* from the arrows of the enemy by teaching us how to posture our lives before God (see Ephesians 6:14–15).

We are all like a bunch of tea bags. What is on the inside really seeps out when we are put into hot water. What comes out of you when stress happens or chaos hits? Do you spill over with the Word of God and the fruit of God's Spirit? Or do you spew venom and words of fear or hatred? Pressures of life are a great test of our inner values and spiritual strength.

I have not always been great at this. I remember being a young athlete and how difficult it was to control my temper. There were times when I thought I was going to lose my testimony over bullies on the court. But over time, God began to teach me how to allow pressures to forge the metal of my armor and practice the art of self-control. Gradually, I began to react less and love more. I played just as hard, but I would not let stress or opposition change my internal peace. Eventually, that training bled over into my relationships, giving me the ability to maintain peace in the midst of pressure.

"But when the Holy Spirit controls our lives he will produce this kind of fruit in us: love, joy, peace, patience, kindness, goodness, faithfulness, gentleness and self-control" (Galatians 5:22–23 TLB).

The proof that your heart is covered by the breastplate of righteousness is seen when your values and motives manifest the fruit of the Spirit in all things, even the worst things. It is simply not possible to do this on your own and in your own emotions. When the Holy Spirit fills you to capacity, however, He empowers you to do what you could never do yourself and strengthens you to think, feel and process through "the mind of Christ" (1 Corinthians 2:16). This is why we cannot conjure up righteousness. It must be released through the power of the Holy Spirit operating in our lives.

Living a righteous life without God is impossible. You cannot do it with your own will or through your own efforts. That is why Jesus died and sent the Holy Spirit to help us live a more holy life. Righteousness is simply living a life of humble worship before God and making His Word the final authority in our lives. It is posturing our lives under the covering of the blood of Jesus and remaining submitted to the voice of the Holy Spirit. Eventually, we should begin to take on His nature, His personality and His character.

"But the Counselor, the Holy Spirit . . . will teach you all things and remind you of everything I have told you," Jesus said (John 14:26 HCSB).

It is the Holy Spirit's job to be a personal trainer who continually reminds us how to stay postured in right standing with God. We may mess up, but I can assure you, the Holy Spirit will remind us that we can do better and nudge us into a better posture that reflects Him.

Jesus continued, "When He comes, He will convict the world about sin, righteousness, and judgment" (John 16:8 HCSB).

The Holy Spirit is not out to scold us, but to mold us into the image of Christ. Ultimately, He is our personal life coach, counselor, comforter, guide, trainer and advocate for living our *best* life. In the end, His goal for you is to hear the Father tell you, "Well done, my good and faithful servant."[5] These are words that Lucifer (Satan) never had the honor of hearing. He thought he was good enough on his own and could exist apart from God. He failed to realize that his powerful reflection was only the result of his humbled posture before God. When that posture changed, and pride entered his spirit, he was banished from heaven for eternity.[6]

The Holy Spirit is your secret weapon to avoid that same mistake. Righteousness is all about posture, not perfection. When

Lucifer's posture shifted toward his own greatness, his pride and his ego began to rule his heart and separated him from the light of the Father.

Putting on the breastplate of righteousness means that you posture yourself with the *truth* of God's Word hidden in your heart so that you can stand against the voice of the enemy. When you do this, God's righteousness becomes your breastplate, the fruit of the Spirit becomes your covering and the arrows or temptations that come against you bounce off without penetrating your heart.

BOOM!—TIME TO REFLECT

When you do an internal audit of your mind, will and emotions, can you see how the enemy tries to distract you from your best life? Is there something or someone that continues to penetrate your heart or steal your joy? What is something you could do today that would help you deepen your relationship with God? What can you do *right now* to reposition your breastplate of righteousness so you can resist the enemy?

Pray this prayer out loud:

Heavenly Father,

I come before You and ask You to help me reposition my breastplate of righteousness. I choose, today, to stand upright before You with an honest and humble heart of worship. I can't be righteous apart from You. Holy Spirit, You are my only hope at living a life that is fully pleasing to the Father. Teach me to be an honorable woman of worship who stands postured with confidence before the Creator of the universe. I commit to study Your Word and practice daily, obeying it in my everyday life. Help me to be more like You. In Jesus' name, Amen.

12

Put On Your Supernatural Nikes

The Shoes of the Gospel of Peace

Suddenly she realized that the right shoes can take you to all the right places.

In 490 B.C., King Darius of Persia invaded Greece and threatened the city of Athens. The Athenians sent their best and fastest long-distance runner, Pheidippides, to Sparta to ask for their help in battle. He ran the full 140 miles to Sparta (two days and two nights) only to find that the Spartans refused to send help until the moon was full. He ran all the way back to Athens with the devastating news.

Meanwhile, the Persians landed on the Greek coast just over 25 miles away. Pheidippides joined the historical race of ten thousand heavily outnumbered Athenian warriors who boldly charged from Athens to Marathon and defeated the Persians in battle. After the victory, Pheidippides was given the grueling task of taking the *good news* of victory all the way back to Athens once again.[1] He was tired and battle weary, but when he finally stumbled back into the city, he mustered up every bit of energy and shouted, "Nike!" (meaning "victory"). Then he collapsed and died.[2]

Pheidippides has been immortalized as the world's first marathon runner. He gave his all to run a race others would never run. *Nike*, which also means "victory," is one of today's most successful shoe brands, fitting athletes for competition around the globe.

What is the *nike* (victory) that you are called to accomplish in your lifetime? Is it a race of men, a race of valor, or is it the quest for eternal peace?

The Good News of Peace

> Therefore put on the full armor of God, so that when the day of evil comes, you may be able to stand your ground, and after you have done everything, to stand. Stand firm then, with the belt of truth buckled around your waist, with the breastplate of righteousness in place, and with your feet fitted with the readiness that comes from the *gospel of peace*.
>
> Ephesians 6:13–15, emphasis added

When Paul spoke about having your feet fitted with the preparation that comes from the Good News of peace, he was offering clear wisdom on how to win the race that would be set before us in this life. Paul's comparison to shoes tells us he knew the journey ahead of us would require a firm-footed foundation so that we might run swiftly in our pursuit to bring peace to the marketplace and to the world around us.

According to an online version of the *Oxford Dictionary*, the word *readiness* means "the state of being fully prepared for something."[3] A ready soldier had to be prepared at all times for surprise attacks or unexpected opposition. That is why his footwear was

139

essential for both offensive pursuits and defensive escapes. Caligae, the legendary heavy-soled boots of Roman soldiers, were studded with nails, much like the cleats that many athletes wear today. The studs helped runners keep a firm grip in combat or competition.[4] If a soldier lost his footing, he lost his ability to stand strong in the heat of battle and maneuver skillfully during the fight.

We live in a culture where the battle for our attention is a slippery slope, and if we lose our focus, we can quickly lose spiritual ground. The world has prioritized money, fame, fortune, social followers, popularity and power as the greatest quest of mankind. All these earthly pleasures, however, merely create a life of imaginary happiness, but they fail to offer lasting peace. When this Scripture speaks to us about being fitted with the readiness or "preparation" that comes from the Good News of peace, it means that there is a life that transcends the fleshly realm of empty promises that so many people strive to conquer.

When we put on the shoes of peace, they will carry us to a place that we could never go in our own strength. Peace supersedes understanding and allows us to rise above the fray and operate on the plane of the supernatural.

"Set your mind on things above, not on earthly things," Paul wrote in Colossians 3:2. When we are fully awakened to the Gospel of peace, our eyes are fixed on heaven's perspective. Satan's attack to overwhelm us with the things of this world no longer penetrates our armor. Instead, our focus shifts to the things of God, and our currency of exchange is out of this world. The more we focus on earthly things, the more depression, anxiety, fear, bitterness and unforgiveness capture our attention. But the more we focus on things that are above, the more we gain firm footing in the race set before us.

I call it the currency of the Kingdom—the economy Larry and I learned to live in when we gave up our titles, time and treasure to God. The currency of the Kingdom cannot be bought by anything of tangible worth on earth. It cannot be achieved by talent, skill or human power. It is not carnal or material. The currency of the Kingdom is worth far more than money can buy, and it is the only currency that heals the hunger and longing within the soul of man.

Kingdom currency is love, joy, peace, patience, kindness, goodness, longsuffering, self-control, forgiveness, generosity, humility and the character of God's nature. This is the economy of heaven and the only currency that will give you access to heavenly abundance and lasting peace. More money, more relationships, more titles, more awards, more followers and more stuff will never be enough to give you the *more* peace you really desire.

Think about how many executives, world leaders and even pastors have fallen prey to a spirit of temptation, sexual immorality or financial manipulation, thinking somehow they could find peace through profits or people. Satan loves when men and women build earthly kingdoms made of earthly treasure. He loves watching good, Christian people grow in earthly power, especially if they lack the currency of heaven. Profits without peace is like a bucket that has a massive hole in the bottom. Enough is never enough. The enemy of lies wants man to suffer in pride because that is the very emotion that caused him to be kicked out of heaven and eternally separated from God's abundance.

Satan knows the more you awaken to the things of God, the more you will operate with the currency of the Kingdom. Your eyes become fixed on higher purposes and Kingdom progress instead of selfish ambitions and monetary gain. Despite the pressures around you, your life begins to magnify the love of God and testify with a peace that passes all understanding. In that state of perfect unity with God's will, you will become a conduit that brings heaven to earth and shines like a light in the darkness. The more you separate yourself from sin, greed and the lusts of the flesh, the more you will grow in power and authority with God.

That is why Satan uses ego and pride as the ally to his strategy against your peace. He whispers to your good-looking co-worker to stay late at work on the very night that your armor is down and your hunger for something more is heightened. His deceptive antics heighten your senses to lust for what you do not have. Or perhaps he uses your late-night research online to pop a vivid image or video across your computer screen that draws you into a world of sexual arousal that temporarily gives you a high that you have been missing. Satan plays on your search for significance by encouraging you to drop your guard and have just one more drink, despite your addictions.

He is a thief. He is a liar. He comes to destroy your peace. And that is why you must always have your feet fit inside spiritual shoes that allow you to run away from the temptations of the flesh. Having your spiritual Nikes on will empower you to flee immorality and pursue peace at all cost.

The list of the many vices or tactics of the enemy are endless, but what is singular is his goal to rob you of your peace by creating a world of suffering and chaos around you. Peace is not a destination, but it is a spiritual attribute that transcends the cravings of this world. It is a currency that can be used to purchase greater things in the Kingdom. It is greater than earthly profitability and brings more fulfillment than power or any position on earth.

Peace over Profits

Imagine you have the choice between two destinies. You can only choose one, and your choice means forsaking the other.

1. The first destiny is a life of *unlimited profits and positional power*. You have everything money can buy. Your existence is defined by form and matter. Homes, cars, shoes, clothes and earthly assets are at your disposal with unlimited access. You work hard for your money, and you are popular, powerful and positioned at the top of the corporate ladder. You are socially followed by millions and

confidently poised with courage. You stand confidently in rooms of power, knowing you have the world in the palm of your hands. Your power is seen in the many companies you create and the transactions you inspire. This, however, is the extent of your worth. Your family pays the price for your hard work, and your health is at risk for the many late nights that demand your attention. You stay in "push" mode but try to use your wealth to take many vacations and live an extravagant life of luxury.

2. The second destiny is a life of *complete peace*. In this life, you have at your disposal everything money cannot buy. You have inner tranquility, harmony, calmness, well-being, contentment, love, humility, patience and a deep and lasting joy. Things of this world do not define you, and so you have very little that money can buy. You are relatively unknown and find little joy in the applause of others, knowing that your life is fully entrusted to the hands of your Creator. Your greatest power is seen in how you reflect God in humility, giving Him glory for the transformational change you bring to others. Your time is spent listening instead of talking, loving instead of feeling a constant need to lead. You are fully present in the conversations before you, and you look deeply into the eyes of those who gain your attention. You are surrounded by the needs of others and yet, somehow, beyond all logic or understanding, you maintain constant peace and have a joy that is undeniable. You don't have much of a material inheritance to leave to your children, but you leave for them a legacy of integrity, love, peace and intimacy with the Holy Spirit.

I know it is easy to see which path we *should* take, but be honest: Which path has our greatest attention? What do you spend more time searching for each day? Are you in "beast-mode" (pursuing success), or do you live in "peace-mode" (seeking the heart of God)?

First Peter 3:11 tells us to "seek peace and pursue it." Unfortunately, that is not the pursuit of the common man, and the result is a generation of restless, socially anxious, depressed, confused and totally stressed-out individuals searching for identity in temporal pleasures that only offer empty promises of peace. Beyond this world of form and matter, there exists a spiritual identity that allows you to transcend this world's suffering and open your heart to let heaven invade your earth. This is the big mystery of the Gospel of peace and what the armor of God is all about.

A Shift in Consciousness

Paul speaks of the armor, not so that you will be weighed down or burdened behind a defense system or a list of rules. Instead, the armor of God is about having a shift in consciousness where you no longer fight battles in the natural realm but instead, you wage war with all of heaven backing you up. This becomes a spiritual force field around you that not only protects, but it also taps you into absolute abundance, peace and authority.

Jesus clearly brought this consciousness of heaven to earth by living among us. He spent three years showing His disciples how to wage war in the Spirit and transcending earth's limitations. He gave a daily "how-to" clinic on being separated from the temptations of the enemy by using God's Word to engage heaven's power on earth. But still, despite His perfect example, the disciples struggled to awaken to this new reality of God's open heavens. Despite the many miracles, walking on water, calming the storms, healing the blind, casting out devils and raising the dead, the disciples still remained locked inside their limited human understanding.

That is why Jesus ascended back into heaven and sent the Holy Spirit of God to live inside us. The Holy Spirit could have continued to reside in tabernacles or costly church buildings, but instead, God sent His Spirit to live in us, bringing the fullness of heaven to earth. That means that when you fully understand the Gospel or "Good News" of peace, you know that the God of heaven lives in you and so does the fruit or manifestation of His Spirit.

Heaven has come to invade your life with God's Spirit. You can live in absolute peace, love and joy and be a conduit of that presence to others even here on earth. When you do, you will truly become enlightened to God's eternal presence in you, and you will run the race that God has set before you.

BOOM!—TIME TO REFLECT

God never promised us a life without storms, but He did give us permission to dance in the rain. That means you can have peace in the midst of chaos, especially when you learn to anchor yourself in the mind of Christ. Tapping into Christ consciousness will be your secret weapon to help you to outwit, outlast and outplay the enemy's plan against your life. He wants you to become distracted by things that will never satisfy the longing in your soul. What are you pursuing most in your life? Has it led you to a life of peace? What can you do today that would help you run with the preparation of peace and stay centered on the mind of Christ?

Pray this prayer out loud:

Heavenly Father,
   I have found myself often distracted by the things of this world. Sometimes it's in the things I read or the people I follow. Sometimes my peace is stolen by the comparisons I make of myself to others. But, God, I know that I could

search the world over and never find the peace that I find only in You. You are my peace. I am complete in You. I lack nothing in You. I have abundance when I rest in You. Holy Spirit, teach me to keep my eyes on what matters most and flood my heart with a peace that passes all understanding, according to Philippians 4:7. In Jesus' name I pray, Amen.

13

Quench the Enemy's Fiery Darts

The Shield of Faith

As she stepped out from the ashes, it was not her loudness of voice that demonstrated power; it was her humbleness of heart that moved mountains.

Whehen I was 28 years old, God opened many doors for me to sing and share my testimony around the world. Soon, I was booked to speak and sing at churches, youth groups, conventions, television stations and stadiums throughout North America and even the world. The more soulful the church, the more I spoke with passion and authority and they would shout me down with their amens and hallelujahs. My speaking became full-on preaching, like a rip-snorting, power-packed Full Gospel preacher with all-out abandonment.

My preaching and my songs were strong and full of authority. When the miracles and signs and wonders took place in our meetings, I was empowered to go even stronger. God showed up, and I was so honored that I kept saying, "Yes, Lord." But, after a year or so, I noticed I could not hit my top two octaves and my voice became more and more raspy every time I would sing or speak. It continued to get worse. Instead of listening to the leading of the Spirit to give my vocal cords much needed rest, I was intent on pressing on.

The next year my travel team (my husband, my mom and my graphic artist) and I traveled to South Africa. I spoke and sang in meetings and in crusades from sunup to sundown until I could barely speak. My "roar" became more like a squeak. I was barely able to utter a word. Despite my vocal struggle, notable miracles were taking place at every service, and the more I witnessed, the more I knew God was using me in such a powerful way. And I just could not stop.

After every service, I would hear the Holy Spirit tell me to rest in between those ministry events, but I just kept speaking and giving those precious people my all. Those dear pastors, church leaders and their own team members were drawing everything out of me, every minute they could. My heart and love for them held me captive to sit with them until after midnight after each public event. They were so hungry to learn, and I was drawing strength from the attention.

When we returned to the United States, I was booked to speak for numerous churches and events across the nation and so my push continued, and my vocal cords suffered the consequences. Every time I saw a blind eye open or a lame person walk, I knew God was using me. But God did not want me addicted to the results; He wanted me submitted to His leading. Instead of obeying that voice to rest, I pressed on with my schedule.

I was asked to speak at The Potter's House in Dallas, where T. D. Jakes is the pastor. It was a dream come true for me, and as I prepared to share my testimony and sing my "Cinderella" song, I knew I was in trouble. My voice was barely a whisper, and I knew I was at the end of my talent's ability to endure. I needed a miracle just to get through those services.

I cried out to God to give me grace for those three services, and if He would, I vowed to check myself in to the Vanderbilt Bill Wilkerson Center, which specializes in treating ear, nose and throat diseases and where so many other professional singers go for vocal therapy and recovery.

I will never forget having the probes sent through my nose and down my throat and hearing the doctor tell me that my vocal cords looked like hamburger meat. I had nodules, bleeding and scar tissue all over my throat. The doctor conveyed that I would need surgery and then undergo months of recovery. He went on to say that I would need to learn how to speak all over again and it would be questionable what my voice strength would be after the surgery. He proceeded to tell me that I needed to give my vocal cords two weeks of complete and absolute vocal rest so that the swelling would go down for the surgery. I thought, *Lord, have mercy! Me? Not speak for two whole weeks?*

My husband, Larry, took my hand gently to comfort me, and together we prayed. In that instant, my spirit was infused with unwavering faith and my spirit became undaunted. I knew that the enemy had tried to kill me as a baby in the area of my lungs and now his attack was on my vocal cords. I realized where I had let the enemy penetrate my armor, and I was ready to do my part in fighting back and winning another victory over the enemy's tactics to take me out.

From that moment forward through the next two weeks, I was silent. I did not say a word. I obeyed the doctor completely and only spoke through writing. During that time, I repented for my disobedience and started posting handwritten Scriptures from God's Word all over my house. Post-it notes were everywhere you could imagine, including doors, windows, desks, car seats, toilets and throughout books and Bibles. I was keeping God's truths before my eyes, day and night.

The enemy tried his best to penetrate my shield of faith with voices of what ifs and tactics of fear, but every time he lied and said I would never sing again, I pulled out God's truth and declared in writing that "He sent His word to heal me."

Two weeks passed, and the prayers of thousands went up before God on my behalf. As I walked back into the doctor's office, I did not know if my voice would work or not. They put the probes back up my nose and down my throat and watched on camera as the test began.

They asked me to say, "Ahh." I did, and a clear sound came out.

They asked me to sing, "He-he-he-he-he." Again, it was perfectly clear.

The nurses called for the doctor, and he stared at the video. Then he asked me to do it again. When he saw it for himself, he called in a group of interns. Again, he asked me to sing small syllables. As they all stood around the monitor screen, I was wondering what was happening.

The doctor, who claimed not to be a man of faith, pushed his chair back and asked me, "Can you please tell me what you did these past two weeks?"

"I obeyed your orders to rest my voice, I prayed, and I posted healing Scriptures all over my home."

"Nothing else?"

"Well, I had a lot of people praying for me."

He shook his head. "Well, I have never seen vocal cords as severely damaged as yours reverse themselves without surgery. And though I do not consider myself a religious man, I would definitely consider this a God factor. Your vocal cords are normal. Now let's train you how to use them effectively and let us explain the importance of vocal rest."

Shield Yourself against Flaming Arrows

Therefore put on the full armor of God, so that when the day of evil comes, you may be able to stand your ground, and after you have done everything, to stand. Stand firm then, with the belt of truth buckled around your waist, with the breastplate of righteousness in place, and with your feet fitted with the readiness that comes from the gospel of peace. In addition to all this, take up the *shield of faith*, with which you can extinguish all the flaming arrows of the evil one.

Ephesians 6:13–16, emphasis added

The shield of faith is an integral part of our armor against the enemy's efforts to destroy our testimony. The King James Version of verse 16 reads, "Above all, taking the shield of faith, wherewith ye shall be able to quench all the fiery darts of the wicked."

By the early days of the Roman empire, each foot soldier carried a *scutum*—a rectangular piece of armor with a large metal knob called a boss in the center. The boss, made of brass, bronze or iron, allowed soldiers to use their shields as an offensive weapon to inflict major blows of force on their opponents. They were also strategical defense shields that protected soldiers from the onslaught of fiery arrows of their enemy. When multiple soldiers took formation side by side, their *scuta* (or shields) became a wall of defense, creating an impenetrable force.[1] This is why I am so passionate about seeing women align side by side in the Body of Christ with their shields of faith in position. They become a mighty force of God that the enemy cannot penetrate. Women in perfect alignment with God's Word can shake nations and protect future generations.

Each of these slightly curved shields measured close to four feet tall and almost three feet wide, making their sheer size a great source of protection from enemies. "When used in combination, scuta provided excellent overhead cover, enabling units to storm fortifications."[2] Likewise, faith is both offensive as well as defensive in power.

Hebrews 11:1 declares, "Now faith is the substance of things hoped for, the evidence of things not seen." The word *substance*

151

can be defined as "ultimate reality that underlies all outward manifestations."[3] Further, the word *evidence* is "something that furnishes proof."[4] So let's rephrase this popular Scripture to say, "Faith is the ultimate reality of things you are hoping for and the proof of the things you have not yet seen."

When you truly have faith, you already see it as reality. You own it as yours. You believe it as ultimate truth. No matter what the bank account says, or the doctors say, or the circumstances show, faith is undaunted, unshakable and unwavering.

Those few weeks of my life could have been filled with fear and doubt anticipating the worst outcome. That would have affected the chemicals in my body and further affected the outcome of my prayers. But instead of believing the report of the doctor, I believed I was healed. I stood on God's Word as the final authority and I was not moved by my circumstances. I, along with my husband and countless others, held up our shields of faith, which moved the enemy out of the way and moved God into rightful position to fulfill His promises toward me.

Let Go of My Ego

Jesus said to his disciples, "Truly I tell you, it is hard for someone who is rich to enter the kingdom of heaven. Again I tell you, it is easier for a camel to go through the eye of a needle than for someone who is rich to enter the kingdom of God." When the disciples heard this, they were greatly astonished and asked, "Who then can be saved?" Jesus looked at them and said, "With man this is impossible, but with God all things are possible."

Matthew 19:23–26

Remember the waffle commercial where everyone rushed to the toaster to get their Eggo waffle, claiming, "Hey, that's mine!"? It is much like the movie *Finding Nemo*, when all the birds rushed

152

after little Nemo as if he would be their dinner entree and chirping, "Mine, mine, mine." This is the cry of ego's insatiable thirst for the self-gratifying pleasures of this world.

During your workday, the enemy is not going to try to penetrate your armor with a bomb or a terrorist attack nearly as often as the attack of your ego. His goal is to shift your posture and corrupt your character, integrity, honesty and honor. His terror or fear tactics are those that are sent to make you feel like you need man's approval, and without it, he makes you feel worthless, impotent, fearful, hopeless or even worse, prideful and hungry for power.

You have heard the story of the "rich young ruler" who walked away sad when Jesus asked him to sell everything and follow Him (see Matthew 19:16–22). Here is a paraphrased version of how this true story might play out in today's society.

A young entrepreneur hits the big time when his start-up tech company goes public. It is fresh money, and so he lives big and others can see his obvious financial success. He attends church regularly on Sundays and even serves on the usher/greeter team on Wednesdays. He seems to be *doing* everything right and is even recognized as a top giver in the church since his newfound riches have given him the ability to give more than most. His social media followers think he is the epitome of success, and they love the material-rich lifestyle he represents in all of his posts. He seems to be living the American dream by all human standards of success. Then one day, he sees Jesus healing people and offering them eternal life. So he steps up and asks Jesus, "Good Teacher, what good thing shall I do that I may have eternal life?" (v. 16 NKJV).

What happens next in Scripture is priceless—literally priceless.

Recognizing the kink in this young entrepreneur's moral armor, Jesus asks him to sell everything—sell his stocks, his home, his Bentley and even the Ferrari—and completely *cash out* his assets and give all of his money to the poor. Jesus asks him to give up his titles, position and public prestige and become His servant for life.

And, pause . . .

The moment of truth is met by an eternity of silence. I can imagine the moments that followed were like listening for a pin to drop. And there it was. The hole in his armor. The weakness to his soul. The access to his heart. Jesus was revealing the young man's posture and what really mattered most in his heart. His true idols of highest worship were not the things of God, but the things of this world. He wanted Jesus to bend the rules for his fleshly lusts and earthly idols.

Jesus took the needle of humility and punched right through the young man's bubble of pride. I can imagine the rich young ruler resolving, "Yeah, well . . . no! I like You, Jesus, but I don't like You *that* much. I mean, You're a good teacher and all, but I don't think that You're the *only* way to eternal life. So yeah . . . I'm out!"

Sounds like modern-day morality: "If it *feels* right, do it. But if it goes against my personal desires, then *no thanks*." As leaders, we strive for perfection, recognition, advancement, achievement, earthly prosperity and other self-gratifying accolades that please our ego. We want to be viewed as "better than most" so we post the "touched-up" pictures, smiling selfies and app-altered images of perfection.

But God sees through all that muck and mire of self-applause. While man scrolls endlessly, looking at the flesh or physical successes of man, God stares deep into the motives of our heart and studies our posture. He is not looking for perfect vessels; He is looking for *yielded vessels* who have put on the breastplate of righteousness so that "no weapon formed against you will succeed" (Isaiah 54:17 HCSB).

"Jesus answered, 'If you want to be perfect, go, sell your possessions and give to the poor, and you will have treasure in heaven. Then come, follow me.' When the young man heard this, *he went away sad*, because he had great wealth" (Matthew 19:21–22, emphasis added).

Jesus revealed the weakness in this young man's armor. His heart was exposed, and his lack of faith revealed. His lips spoke of honor, but his actions unmasked his pride: "These people honor me with their lips, but their hearts are far from me. They worship me in vain; their teachings are merely human rules" (Matthew 15:8–9).

As a Christian in the marketplace, your breastplate of righteousness is what gives you protection and confidence to fight battles in the Spirit that others are afraid to fight. The confidence of being in right relationship with God will empower you to pray with boldness, knowing that you are rightly positioned as a fully approved agent of change in this world. Position, prosperity and rank do not impress God. Instead, it is the heart of faith and righteousness that moves mountains and triggers miracles from heaven.

The rich young ruler did not have a money issue. He had a faith issue. His trust or faith was in his riches, so when Jesus told him to sell it all and follow Him, it was a test of his faith, not his fortune. Faith is the key to unlock the miraculous. God is not moved by the magnitude of your circumstances, but He *is* greatly moved by the depth of your faith.

Obedience Precedes the Miraculous

"Do not fear, only believe."

Mark 5:36 ESV

Two sales executives from the shoe industry were sent to explore a possible emerging market in Asia. Both were eager to seize any opportunities and were more than willing to take the assignment. A month later, both executives returned with a full report of their findings. Both agreed that rarely did they find anyone in the country wearing shoes.

The first executive was frustrated by the wasted journey and reported there was no demand for shoes, and therefore no sales opportunity. The second executive had a much different outlook. He was full of enthusiasm, reporting that since no one had shoes, there was a virtually untapped market and they should start shipping immediately.[5] Both executives were privy to the same outcome. While one saw opportunity, the other only saw obstacles. Astute leadership begins with adopting a mindset that focuses on what "could be" rather than what currently is.

> *You see things; and you say, "Why?" But I dream things that never were; and I say, "Why not?"*[6]

The power of positive thinking rests on the backbone of spiritual faith. Where the ceiling of positive thinking ends, the limitless possibilities of faith begins. The enemy of your destiny is not moved by your dreams or successes, but he is devastated by your faith.

Hebrews 11:6 teaches us that "without faith it is impossible to please God, because anyone who comes to God must believe that He exists and that He rewards those who earnestly seek him."

Faith is putting your absolute trust in God, no matter what your circumstances may look like and no matter what the cost. Faith demands a right relationship with God. It requires focus on what can be and not merely what is. Faith is the umbilical cord of how heaven reaches earth and miracles are manifested in our reality.

God honors faith. Words alone do not change spiritual environments—faith does. And "faith comes by hearing" God's will as it is written in His Word (Romans 10:17 NKJV). Scripture reveals God's will, and the more we know Scripture, the more we can use it in prayer against the enemy.

Jesus said, "Truly I tell you, if you have faith as small as a mustard seed, you can say to this mountain, 'Move from here to there,' and it will move. *Nothing will be impossible for you*" (Matthew 17:20, emphasis added). If God tells you to trust Him with your finances and you continue to worry, you are proving your lack of faith. If God asks you to do something that seems *crazy* to the natural eye, but you do it in obedience to His Word, rest assured that He will work it out and your obedience will come with great reward.

The disciples proved a *lack* of faith when they freaked out on the boat in the middle of the storm. Jesus was on that same boat, in that same storm, sound asleep. Why? Jesus did not have a faith issue. His absolute trust was in God, His Father. When we obey without fear or worry, we are saying, *God, I believe in You. I trust that You are able to do exceedingly, abundantly far above all I could ask or think. Even if I look like a fool, I put my trust in You to work this out for my good.*

The shield of faith is an essential part of our defense strategy against the enemy. And usually when God asks us to do something in complete faith, it will be opposite the standards or practices of what is considered "normal" around us. He asked Noah, by faith, to build a ship in the middle of a field, even though there was no rain or even a history of rain.

Shadrach, Meshach and Abednego stood firm and unwavering when King Nebuchadnezzar attacked their values and beliefs because their faith shielded them from the potential harm of the enemy. Their refusal to bow down to the cultural idols of their time said, *Our God is bigger than your gods. Our God has a better outcome for our future than the false gods and their fake rituals. Our God is fully able to deliver us from death, and even if He doesn't, He can raise us back from the dead.*

The list of the faithful goes on and on. No doubt, your life, your job and your vision will demand that you choose a master. Will you serve the idols or voices of this world, or will you surrender your will to that of the Father and choose to live by faith?

BOOM!—TIME TO REFLECT

What are you praying for today? What do you need God to do on your behalf that seems impossible at this moment? What area of your life do you need to increase your faith and elevate your expectancy?

Pray this prayer out loud:

Holy Spirit,
Come now and flood my heart. I want to know You more.
I want to have faith that can move mountains, and I know
that You, living in me, are the key to that kind of faith. You
were with Christ. Be with me. Be my teacher, my counselor
and my guide. Help me turn from disbelief and teach me
how to have audacious, relentless, unyielding faith. I release
fear and doubt from this day forward, and I cling to a firm
understanding that with You, God, anything is possible. I
believe and I receive You now. Amen.

14

Protect Your Head in Battle

The Helmet of Salvation

No longer playing the role of a victim, she grabbed her helmet and headed into battle to save her kingdom.

When my daughter, Alexia, was still an infant, I was traveling two to three times a month to different states, speaking and singing for large events in stadiums across the nation. On one occasion, I was preparing for an upcoming trip when I noticed that she had a runny nose.

Now, let me preface this story to say that I am one of those homeschool health-nut moms that had my kids "naturally," avoided epidurals and immunizations and even let our kids "burn out" a fever to build their immune systems. My epidural-loving girlfriends thought I was crazy and to this day do not fully understand why I would want to endure pain when a simple needle could make it all go away. But twelve months before I got pregnant with our son, Payton, we met a sweet couple with five children and they advised us of the many benefits to living a chemical-free lifestyle, and so

. . . we became that family that avoided flu shots, immunizations and even Advil, if at all possible.

But the day we noticed Alexia's runny nose, another mom looked at her in my arms and said, "Oh, dear. You can't fly with her having congestion. The cabin pressure could blow her eardrums."

It is amazing how fast the opinions of others can make you do things you would not usually do yourself. I packed both kids into the car and headed to the clinic. When we arrived, they put us in a room, checked her heartbeat, ears, and basic vitals and then we waited for the doctor to see us.

Suddenly, the doctor and another man in a white coat came into the room and said they needed to take her immediately for further testing. Their tone of voice was particularly stressful, so I said, "Is everything okay?" They said she was carrying the symptoms for meningitis, and that they wanted to do a spinal tap to be certain.

My heart sank. I was in shock. "I don't think that's necessary," I said. "I only came in because she's had a runny nose and I wanted you to check her ears to be sure we can fly with her."

They said they understood, but her symptoms were very alarming.

Without hesitation, I called my husband, who was out of town at the time. When I told him what they were saying, I could not stop crying as the pressure of making that decision alone was overwhelming at the moment.

He agreed that the spinal tap seemed sudden and extreme but told me, "Baby, I'm not there to see her. I trust you in the decision you make." Then he prayed that I would have the "mind of Christ" (1 Corinthians 2:16 KJV), and a peace came over my heart.

When the doctor returned, I told her that I wanted to take 24 hours to see if Alexia's runny nose cleared up before my flight. She advised me that due to the severity of what they were seeing, she would have to ask me to sign papers that would release them from liability or cause of death. I agreed to sign whatever they needed and headed home with babies in tow.

The next day, Alexia's little nose was still runny, but this time she was crying *a lot*. That is when I noticed something was bothering her in her mouth, and when I pressed on her gums, there it was—her first tooth. She was teething, not suffering from meningitis. But had I listened to the people around me more than the voice within me, I would have been influenced to make a very unsafe decision.

The more I took time to re-center my mind on Christ, the more I was able to put on the helmet of salvation and see, hear and discern clearly what I should do in that moment. As I prayed and asked the Holy Spirit for wisdom, despite the pressure of the moment, the voices of the doctors and others faded, and the voice of truth became resoundingly clear. This is why having the mind of Christ is key to being able to be a good steward of our children's lives as well as a steward of everything God entrusts to us.

Guard Your Command Center

> Therefore put on the full armor of God, so that when the day of evil comes, you may be able to stand your ground, and after you have done everything, to stand. Stand firm then, with the belt of truth buckled around your waist, with the breastplate of righteousness in place, and with your feet fitted with the readiness that comes from the gospel of peace. In addition to all this, take up the shield of faith, with which you can extinguish all the flaming arrows of the evil one. And take the *helmet of salvation*, and the sword of the Spirit, which is the word of God.
>
> Ephesians 6:13–17, emphasis added

The greatest attack of the enemy will always be waged on the battlefield of the mind. The voices that play in our head will determine the choices we make, the alignments we create and the idols we worship. When Paul spoke of the helmet of salvation, he

161

was stressing the importance of guarding the command center of our lives and refusing to let outside voices or forces take us off course.

The Roman helmet (*galea*), like helmets today, protected the head from injury.[1] The helmet was the last, but certainly not the least, of the armor plates that a soldier would put on before battle. The helmet protects the head, the brain and the command center of all vital organs. The broad-brimmed gladiator's helmet, with its pierced visor, also protected the face and neck.[2] These are the gateway centers to our vision, our focus and our pursuits.

When we put on the helmet of salvation, we tap into the mind of Christ, who sees what the Father sees, hears what the Father hears and obeys what the Father commands. We must consider it our very own virtual reality headset that taps us into divine wisdom almost instantly through the "mind of Christ":

> "What no eye has seen, what no ear has heard, and what no human mind has conceived"—the things God has prepared for those who love him—these are the things God has revealed to us by his Spirit. . . . "Who has known the mind of the Lord so as to instruct him?" But we have the *mind of Christ*.
>
> 1 Corinthians 2:9–10, 16, emphasis added

Even in moments when we have to make important decisions for our families, who you are listening to most will determine what you value greatest. But hearing what to do is often the easy part.

Obeying, on the other hand, is where it gets tricky. If everyone around you is going in a different direction and you know God is telling you to go the other way, obedience requires faith, courage and confidence. Swimming upstream is a challenge. It is so easy just to coast downstream with the crowd. But like a salmon swimming upstream, valuable duplication and legacy happen for those willing to go against the flow, face their fears and press on.

Stop, Drop and Roll

As you can imagine, after having a house fire, there are many things we learned that we have since passed on to others. One was to know that if your home is on fire and you have retrieved your most valuable assets, let it burn. Trying to build around a partially burned structure took twice as long as it would have if it had burned to the slab. Another lesson we learned is that firefighters love fires.

When the fire was fully extinguished, we had time to sit and chat with the young firemen who lay exhausted on our front lawn. I asked one of them, "How does it feel when you hear that alarm go off?"

"Well, I know it sounds crazy," he said, "but it's what we live for. We don't want to sit around the firehouse just waiting or sleeping. We signed up to fight fires! So, when a fire alarm goes off, our adrenaline peaks and we are ready to roll!"

Have you ever heard of the fire strategy "Stop, Drop and Roll"? Basically, if you found yourself on fire, the lesson taught us, as kids, to stop, drop to the ground and roll till the fire was extinguished. This is a great life hack for keeping your mind set on the things of God, as well. If you find your mind in flames of fury, fear or frustration, this will help you regain the mind of Christ in any situation.

1. Stop

Do not allow yourself to stay in a moment of anxiety. Stop and silence the voices in your head. Close your eyes and take a giant breath in and imagine taking in the fullness of God's character, including the fruit of His Spirit, which is love, joy, peace, patience, kindness, etc.

2. Drop

Let go of the stress, anxiety, critical opinions, frustrations, fear and worry. Do this by exhaling with great force. Inhale the peace and love of God again, and exhale the cares of this world. Do

163

this at least three times or until you feel a physical shift in your mindset take place. Let go of every thought, emotion, diagnosis, worry or fear, and place it into the hands of the Creator of the universe immediately (see 1 Corinthians 10:3–5).

3. Roll

Literally and physically turn around. Do an about-face. Force your body into a physical 180-degree shift. The goal is to get the funk of whatever you are facing off your life. I have even had women lie on the ground and roll over in a state of rage or anger so as to disrupt the emotional state that is holding them captive. This may seem ridiculous, but you must take your mind and your body under the authority of Christ and re-center your helmet of saving grace.

The battles we face are *never* about money, position, diagnosis or even people—they are about hearing and obeying God's promises so we can defeat the enemy at his own mind game. The helmet of salvation is our greatest guard against the enemy's voices of fear, rejection, ego, pride, bitterness, offense or greed. He wants to keep blinders on us to keep us from seeing into the future of what God has in store. Instead, he comes to paralyze us in a moment of stress and hold us in a state of mediocrity.

If He Says It, Obey It

> "For God so loved the world that He gave His only begotten Son, that whoever believes in Him should not perish but have everlasting life. For God did not send His Son into the world to condemn the world, but that the world through Him might be saved."
>
> John 3:16–17 NKJV

When we hear the voices of defeat, confusion or desperation screaming in our ears, we know it is time to pick up the Word of

God and meditate on the truth behind our circumstances. When the devil tries to remind us of the failures in our past, we simply put on the helmet of salvation and remind him of his devastating future. The helmet of salvation is the confidence that comes with knowing that Jesus paid a price for our eternal victory by sacrificing His life on the cross. Jesus, the Lamb slain for our future, gives us the authority of a *lion* to wage war on the enemy.

It may seem like there is little you can do about the stress or mental fatigue that comes with being a woman, a mom, a leader and a friend. The truth is, the bills are not going to stop coming, your job and family will continue to demand more than it seems you have to offer, and even well-meaning friends will unknowingly suck the life out of you if you let them. But that is life. You cannot change the world around you, but you *can* protect the world within you by always wearing your helmet of salvation and maintaining the mind of Christ. People and pressures can wreak havoc on a mind that is not centered on the truth of God's Word.

On my second CD, *Be a Champion*, I wrote and recorded a song called "Guard Your Mind." One of the lines says, "Feed your mind with faith; believe and never doubt. For what your heart takes in is what comes pouring out."[3] This is *so* true. What we spend the majority of our time watching, listening to, reading or meditating upon will be the very fragrance or ether we emit emotionally to others. It is very difficult to maintain a positive mental attitude when you hang out with negative people. One very important and practical step in keeping your helmet of salvation firmly fitted on your head is to monitor whom you are spending most of your time with.

Perhaps you have heard it said, "Hang out with chickens and you will forever peck the ground but hang out with eagles and one day you'll fly!" Proximity and associations are major contributors to what type of mindset you maintain on a daily basis. The closer you are to God's Word, God's people, God's community and God's will, the more you will maintain the mind of Christ.

The more you hang out with the world, watch worldly entertainment, listen to worldly music and maintain worldly ideals, the more you will feel the dark pressures and depression of the world caving in around you.

The attacks of the enemy are always designed for fatality, and Satan knows that if he can win the battle of the mind, he can control our choices. This was the strategy that gave him the temporary victory in the Garden of Eden. It was a form of mind control, and for a season, it won him the keys of the earth. His mental manipulation over Adam and Eve is the same mind game he plays on women today. He wants women to look at his delicacies, his power, his control, his fashions and his temptations. And he wants you to believe that you would be a better god of your choices than the Creator of the universe. He is the great deceiver.

But when you, as a woman of God, recognize that a mind stayed upon Christ is a mind fully persuaded for Kingdom purposes, you can make critical decisions that lead to greater abundance and peace. Once you are fully covered by the armor of God, you become Satan's worst nightmare.

BOOM!—TIME TO REFLECT

It is no secret that we have a real enemy and he wants to render you helpless and ineffective in your role as a Warrior Queen for the Kingdom of God. His tactics have never changed. He still uses distraction and mental manipulation to tempt you to move outside of God's will and to steal your peace. But God has given you the helmet of salvation to protect you from the strategies of the enemy. Have you noticed how the enemy tries to invade your mind and steal your focus? What Scripture can you meditate upon that will act as a helmet of protection over your mind, will and emotions?

Pray this prayer out loud:

Dear God,

In Isaiah 26:3, You said that You would keep me in perfect peace if my mind is stayed upon You. I want to hear You say, "Well done" more than anything in my life. I want to honor You with my thoughts and glorify You with my choices. As I meditate upon Your Word, give me ears to hear and eyes to see into the hidden mysteries of Your will. Teach me, Holy Spirit, to have the mind of Christ. In Jesus' name, Amen.

15

Queen, Grab Your Sword

The Sword of the Spirit

She wasn't looking for her crown; she was looking for her sword.

I remember the first girl my son declared he really "liked." She was such a pretty girl but came with a lot of emotional pain and unresolved baggage. He met her at church, and while she was a kind and sweet-hearted girl, something in my spirit said, *Not yet!* It was so clear in my spirit that the relationship, as innocent as it was, would be a distraction to his sixteen-year-old mind, but I knew I could not go about the situation in a "normal" way. Instead, I asked him to pray about whether or not she would really be a candidate for his "God list" of a wife. At first, he acted as if he had not heard me, and I could tell his heart was already getting hooked and he did not want anything to do with my opinion.

So I served notice on the enemy that in order to get to my son's heart with a distraction, he would have to go through me and my sword. I prayed, interceded and waged spiritual war on behalf of my son's heart for two weeks. I did not have to say much to him after that because the Holy Spirit did the talking for me. Payton, my son, began to see little issues of integrity and character flaws that started to appear. Soon, he kindly told her that he needed to refocus, and *boom*, she was gone. It was so clear that, while I am sure God will mold her into a beautiful wife for someone, at that time, for my son, she was a distraction. I had to stand guard as a momma bear and prevent the enemy from creeping in and capturing a knight in my kingdom.

The Sword of God's Word

> Therefore, put on the full armor of God, so that when the day of evil comes, you may be able to stand your ground, and after you have done everything, to stand. Stand firm then, with the belt of truth buckled around your waist, with the breastplate of righteousness in place, and with your feet fitted with the readiness that comes from the gospel of peace. In addition to all this, take up the shield of faith, with which you can extinguish all the flaming arrows of the evil one. Take the helmet of salvation and the *sword of the Spirit*, which is the word of God.
>
> Ephesians 6:13–17, emphasis added

Paul knew the suffering and opposition that come with fulfilling one's purpose on earth, so he made sure young Timothy knew how to gear up for battle. The first five parts of the armor of God mentioned in Ephesians—the belt, breastplate, shoes, shield and helmet—are primarily defensive in nature. All were vital for protection. If you are a Christ follower and have said yes to your mandate to *go* into your world or marketplace and take the Good News of Jesus there, then you will undoubtedly need protection.

But winning a war not only takes a good defensive strategy—you have to get up, face the fire and fight. That requires having weapons for offensive battle. Can you imagine a soldier carefully putting on each piece of armor to protect himself and then running into battle without a weapon? That would be suicide. God is not merely wanting us protected from harm; He wants us equipped to win. The sword of the Spirit is a crucial weapon in our arsenal because it empowers us to attack.

Ancient Roman soldiers wielded double-edged swords known as *gladii*. In the hands of a skillful and trained warrior, the *gladius* was a fearsome weapon. With a heavy blade measuring 18 to 24 inches long, this infantry weapon was designed for close combat on the frontlines after soldiers hurled javelins at the enemy.[1] Swords pierce and penetrate. They cut to the bone. God refers to His Word as a sword in Hebrews 4:12 (NKJV): "For the word of God is living and powerful, and sharper than any two-edged sword, piercing even to the division of soul and spirit, and of joints and marrow, and is a discerner of the thoughts and intents of the heart."

The sword of the Spirit cuts through the smoke and mirrors of our lives, our ego, selfishness and pride, and reveals the deeper intention or motives of our hearts. We can hide from others, but we cannot hide from God. When we use the Word of God as a sword against the enemy, we will discover that God has already won the battle for us. When we use the Word of God as a mirror to our own soul, it pierces through the bondage of our own sin and breaks every chain off our life. When we use it to protect our family, we serve notice to the kingdom of darkness that he is messing with the wrong queen and her kingdom.

Rocky vs. Drago

Jesus, full of the Holy Spirit, left the Jordan and was led by the Spirit into the wilderness, where for forty days he was tempted by the devil. He ate nothing during those days, and at the end of them he was hungry. The devil said to him, "If you are the Son of God, tell this stone to become bread."

Luke 4:1–3

Jesus gave us a perfect example of how to use the sword of the Spirit or Word of God against the enemy's opposition. Jesus was tired, hungry and probably emotionally drained when Satan attacked Him in the desert.

The battle between Jesus and Satan was like the battle in the epic movie *Rocky IV*, where the underdog, Rocky Balboa, is up against the Russian giant, Drago. It seemed like Rocky was out for the count. He was lying on the mat, and it appeared that the fight was over. But then, Rocky got back up and continued to fight with a resilience that was unstoppable. Punch after punch the two battled it out, until finally, Rocky went into a different level of power and became relentless in his attack and took out the infamous Drago to win the championship.

Satan knew full well that Jesus was the only Son of God, and yet his cunning and derogatory words, "If you are the Son of God" (Luke 4:3, 9), were like direct blows to Jesus' claims of authority. Satan always tries to trigger our ego and test our ability to get us to debate our faith as if it were in question.

"And Satan said, 'Tell this stone to become bread'" (v. 3). This was a test of the flesh trying to get Jesus to succumb to His earthly hunger and use His gifts for personal satisfaction. But Jesus fights back with the Word of God by saying, "It is written, 'Man shall not live by bread alone, but by every word that proceeds from the mouth of God'" (Matthew 4:4 NKJV).

Then in round two, Satan takes Jesus up on a mountaintop and shows Him all the kingdoms of the world and says, "All this authority I will give You, and their glory; for this has been delivered to me, and I give it to whomever I wish. Therefore, if You will worship before me, all will be Yours" (Luke 4:6–7 NKJV).

171

Satan was using low blows by trying to attack Jesus' ego and the human thirst for power, but Jesus, again, used the sword of the Spirit to fight back, saying, "Get behind Me, Satan! For it is written, 'You shall worship the LORD your God, and Him only you shall serve'" (v. 8 NKJV).

Round three and Satan punches through to the heart of the Kingdom and takes Jesus to the pinnacle of the temple and says, "If You are the Son of God, throw Yourself down from here. For it is written: 'He shall give His angels charge over you, to keep you,' and, 'In their hands they shall bear you up, lest you dash your foot against a stone'" (vv. 9–10 NKJV).

But Jesus, again, takes the sword of the Spirit and says to him, "It has been said, 'You shall not tempt the LORD your God.'" (v. 12 NKJV).

In every attempt, Satan was trying to get Jesus to shift His worship from the throne of God to the deception of rebellion that caused Lucifer's original fallout. It was also the same temptation that He used on Adam and Eve in the garden. But Jesus proved to us that, with the Holy Spirit, it is possible to defeat Satan in every battle and win over temptation.

On Guard!

In 1891, C. H. Spurgeon delivered a sermon entitled "The Sword of the Spirit," in which he said,

> To be a Christian is to be a warrior. The good soldier of Jesus Christ must not expect to find ease in this world: it is a battlefield. Neither must he reckon upon the friendship of the world; for that would be enmity against God. His occupation is war. . . . The Holy Spirit has proclaimed war, and wields a two-edged sword. The Holy Spirit wields no other sword but the Word of God . . . which contains the utterances of God's mouth, [and] is the one weapon which the Holy Ghost elects to use for his warlike purposes.[2]

Ladies, it is time to stop whining about our issues and start warring on behalf of our families and our futures. The way to do this is to pick up our swords and fight. How? By reading, meditating on and memorizing the Word of God till it pours out of our spirits like living water. It is not enough to go to church, listen to a preacher talk about Scripture. We must *know* Scripture and wield it like a weapon against the enemy.

Have you ever felt like you have taken blow after blow and that the enemy has left you lifeless and exhausted on a mat of suffering? Well, girlfriend, listen to me now. Get up! It is not over. You have more fight in you. You have an army of women warriors interceding for you right now, and you are *fueled by fire*. You are powerful beyond words, and your worth is far greater than any treasure on earth.

Give the devil your best shot. Resist him with the Word of God and he must flee. Even if you start with only one Scripture, say it over and over and over again as if you are swinging your sword with power and might. Say, "I can do all things through Christ who gives me strength" (Philippians 4:13 BSB). Say it over and over again with passion as if you were using those words to punch the devil in the face.

Moms, the next time you have a situation you know needs prayer, win with more than words—win with your sword. When you have a child who comes home with a bad attitude or a friend you know is not good for their future, don't whine . . . *win*. Go to your war room, take out your sword and fight. Resist the devil with the Word of God, not with mere words from your flesh. God's Word has miraculous force to penetrate what human words or intellect will never do.

I have seen some of the most miraculous things occur in the lives of those I love, not because I talked about their situation, but because I took out my sword and declared and decreed change in that situation according to the Word of God.

The world says, "Kids these days are disrespectful." The Word says, "My children will rise and call me blessed" (see Proverbs 31:28).

The world says, "Cancer is an incurable epidemic." The Word says, "The name of Jesus is above every name [including cancer]" (see Philippians 2:9).

The doctor might say, "You will always be bipolar." The Word says, "I will be transformed by the renewing of my mind" (see Romans 12:2).

What or whom you put your trust in will determine how you fight your battles. If your trust is in doctors, they will be your highest opinion of authority. If you put your trust in politics or media, the nightly news will govern your decisions. If you only look at the current behaviors of your family, you might believe they are a lost cause. If you take the Word of God, however, and apply it as a sword to those issues, you will cut through the mistruths and see that God has already fought this battle. And He is asking you to take up your sword and agree with His victory.

BOOM!—TIME TO REFLECT

Some people use God's Word less as a sword and more like a board—a way to hit others and cast judgment on them, a tool of division and discord. But a sword is a spiritual weapon that penetrates spiritual territory and should give you the advantage you need to slay giants fighting against you. Not physical giants, but spiritual opposition standing in the way of your ultimate peace. In the face of opposition, how can you apply God's Word to your circumstances today? What are three Scriptures you can use, starting today, that can penetrate the kingdom of darkness?

Pray this prayer out loud:

Hi God,

It's me again. This time I am standing in the need of great wisdom and strength. I sense You calling me into a deeper place of servitude that will require more courage than I've ever had before. I am growing stronger and stronger every day, and I choose, now, to raise my sword in faith. Lord, use me, mold me, strengthen me and empower me to be Your vessel of truth to the world around me. I am ready to advance into whatever it is You are calling me to do. I am not afraid. I choose to believe that You plus me is a majority, and together, we've already won this battle. In Jesus' name, Amen.

part four

AWAKENING TO YOUR DIVINE PURPOSE

awake (verb):
to become conscious
or aware of something[1]

16

Queens with Fragrance

The fragrance of her humility was even stronger than the beauty of her appearance.

One of my favorite stories of risk-taking, mountain-moving, world-changing women in the Bible is that of Queen Esther. She was just a peasant girl with no royal lineage. Most certainly, she had dreams of her own. Dreams of falling in love, a sacred wedding, her first kiss and dreams of her dearest friends and family attending their wedding feast. Suddenly, she was captured by soldiers, kidnapped of sorts, and whisked away, being told she would never go back to the life she once dreamed possible. And while some young royals would dream of a night with the king, the pageant Esther was being forced to enter would mean the death of her purity, the end of her sacred honor and the last moments of the life she hoped she would live.

Esther was not just being kidnapped by godless men, but the God of the universe was watching, and for some reason, He let it happen. Where was God in that moment? Why didn't He stop it? Why would He let Esther be taken by such a pagan empire?

Could it be true that God saw beyond the moment of suffering and had a plan for Esther's story that would supersede her pain? Could that same God of Esther have seen beyond the suffering of His Son on the cross, knowing the ending of His story would be victory and not death?

Esther was not kidnapped in a sense; she was chosen. Her dramatic shift of scripts was about to give her a story that would empower her to shift the future destiny of the children of Israel. Esther was being stripped of her comfort zone, and her only hope of survival was to take on a completely different mindset than she had been raised to embrace.

Imagine if I asked you to enter a local pageant starting tomorrow. For most of us, we would give an abrupt, "No way. Not going to happen. Thank you, but no thank you!" And assume you had never been in a pageant, nor had you ever dreamed that would be how God decided to use you in this world. Would you say yes? Would you put on that swimsuit or evening gown and parade in front of the nation's top leaders? Okay, if you have not thrown the book at me yet, keep imagining the crazy nature of this story. If that thought is not awkward enough, imagine if I told you that you did not have a choice. Whether you wanted to go or not, you are going to have to smile as if your life depended on it. You are grabbed by soldiers and taken to a massive palace, stripped of your identity, taken from your family and held hostage for months.

This is exactly what happened to Esther, and not only did it come as a surprise, but it violated everything she was taught to respect and hold dear in her life. Oh, how many women I have met who have been violated, stripped, manipulated and used outside of their will. Many have been paraded, prodded, tortured and even made to believe this is all they were good for in this world. But Esther's story gives us a beautiful example of turning a mess into a message.

I am sure there were hours, days and even weeks that Esther brewed, mourned and relented over the injustice of what happened to her. She probably cried herself to sleep at night wondering, *Why, God, why? Where were You? Why didn't You rescue me? Why didn't You step in and shield me from this nightmare? It's so unfair. I did nothing to deserve this.*

Scripture does not reveal all of Esther's emotions or sorrow, but what we do read is the shift that ultimately takes place in her perspective. Esther was in a mess. She was about to become used and potentially very damaged. But even in the horrific details of her kidnapping, God had a plan. The peasant girl of little acclaim was about to be turned into one of the most significant women in Jewish history. At some point in her tragedy, Esther decided to turn pain into a superpower that would change the world.

Esther had to have a total mindset reset to move beyond, *Oh, woe is me!* into, *Why not me? Why not now? Why not use this mess and turn it into a mountain-moving message that sets my people free?* To move from broken to brazen, Esther had to be stripped of her former way of thinking. She had to forgive her abusers. She had to embrace the circumstances that happened to her so that God could flow through her to greater humanity. She had to take on a new perspective about love, life and servitude, and she had to submit to change. She had to let go of her selfish ambitions and put on her strategic mindset so she could outwit, outlast and eventually outmaneuver the enemy.

"Each girl's turn came to go in to King Xerxes after she had completed the twelve months of prescribed beauty treatments— six months' treatment with oil of myrrh followed by six months with perfumes and various cosmetics" (Esther 2:12–14 MSG).

When the time came for her preparation treatments, Esther had to submit to beauty treatments that would remove from her all marketplace odors, habits and any simpleton thinking that would cause her to appear "normal" or that of a peasant woman. This was no easy task. Esther had no royal training, nor was she taught the many protocols of the palace that she would one day represent. She had to undergo twelve months of intense beauty treatments that would cause her to be "refragranced" with the perfumes that most pleased the king.

In the days of Esther, women in consideration for the role of the queen first had to smell like the king's choice oils, and then she had to dress for the kingdom in choice garments. Immediately following her royal beauty treatments, she would be offered access to the royal wardrobe. There, she could choose to clothe herself in any garment, jewelry or fashionable accessory she desired to wear for her one night with the king. If he liked the presentation she offered, she could be chosen as his next queen. Then, as each girl's turn came for spending the night with King Ahasuerus, "she was given her choice of whatever clothing or jewelry she wanted to take from the harem" to enhance her beauty (Esther 2:13 NLT).

Esther represents the process of transformation that we, as women, must submit to if we truly want to rule and reign in a power that is greater than human understanding. To be fueled by the fire of God's Spirit will mean that we must allow God to take us through a metamorphosis out of the old life we once knew and into a transfiguration of becoming more like Christ. To carry the fragrance of a queen, we must spend time in the presence of the King of kings.

The Scent of Heaven

Ahh . . . the *smell* of a queen. She is arrayed with beauty, but her presence is what shifts the atmosphere. She carries the fragrance that most pleases her king, and her nobility is like a thermostat of change that has the power to shift every room in which she enters. She is poised with humility and fortified with strength that comes from knowing the power and authority of the throne she represents. She is not searching for approval, for she has already been approved. This mental positioning is a queen's greatest strength. She is backed by the Kingdom of God, a kingdom far greater than herself. And with such power comes great responsibility.

Ladies, this is the confidence we can have when we know we are loved, adored and made royal by the King of kings. When we carry the fragrance of our King, Jesus, we carry His character, His compassion, His humility and His power into every room we enter. We move from being mere mortal ladies into being women of worth and of Kingdom power.

> So I say, walk by the Spirit, and you will not gratify the desires of the flesh. For the flesh desires what is contrary to the Spirit, and the Spirit what is contrary to the flesh. They are in conflict with each other, so that you are not to do whatever you want. But if you are led by the Spirit, you are not under the law. The acts of the flesh are obvious: sexual immorality, impurity and debauchery; idolatry and witchcraft; hatred, discord, jealousy, fits of rage, selfish ambition, dissensions, factions and envy; drunkenness, orgies, and the like. I warn you, as I did before, that those who live like this will not inherit the kingdom of God.
>
> Galatians 5:16–23

What pleases our King most is the sweet-smelling aroma of a woman lathered in the fruit of His Spirit and clothed in compassion, mercy, tenderness, wisdom and grace.

What fragrance do you wear most on a daily basis? What is the ether or scent that permeates the rooms you enter? Do you carry the scent of heaven, which is love, joy, peace, patience, kindness, goodness, faithfulness, gentleness and self-control? Or are you still lathered in the painful memories of your past? Do you smell of gossip, envy, anger, hatred, bitterness, greed, unforgiveness and shame? These odors are a stench to the King's nostrils and are peasant characteristics that have no place in the palace of the King.

What are the external garments that you have chosen to enhance your beauty? What cloaks your soul on a daily basis? What are the attitudes, thoughts and emotions you adorn yourself with that you have chosen as jewelry or fashion? When others see you, do they see a woman caught up in a worldview, clothed in earthly priorities and popular attitudes, or do they see you cloaked in the fabric of heaven and arrayed with a rare eternal beauty?

Clothed with Humility and Grace

Since God chose you to be the holy people he loves, you must clothe yourselves with tenderhearted mercy, kindness, humility, gentleness, and patience. . . . Above all, clothe yourselves with love, which binds us all together in perfect harmony.

Colossians 3:12–14 NLT

We live in a society that tries to make women believe that power comes from positional rank, popular brands, gender equality, human rights, feminist marches and sexual promiscuity. But this is far from the truth of what God describes as the heavenly design for female honor, excellence and success.

The enemy of lies wants women to believe that in order to have power or acceptance on earth, they must bow to his voice of manipulation that says,

Give up your righteousness so you can achieve the world's respect. If the world loves you, you will have the power you really want. Serving God alone can't bring you the accolades you desire. Why let God make all of the choices in your life? Who says you can't be the author of your womb and the navigator of your future?

Why give up your right to a God who could not possibly have time to consider every detail of your life? And why forgive the people who have hurt you? Instead, prove them wrong.

Let success be your equalizer that shows them they messed with the wrong woman. Power comes through progress, not posture. Why bow yourself in worship to God when I am offering you the world? Spend the most of your time honing your talents and perfecting your skills so that one day the world will love you, praise you and adore your greatness!

This is the fruit of deception that the enemy wants us to eat. He wants women to believe that their power, talent and acceptance is all that. He tries to convince us to mask our spirituality with conformity. He tells us that if we speak out for God's Kingdom, we might lose our jobs, be ridiculed, suffer persecution and even live without public acceptance. But by listening to his lies that you must blend into the world's mindset, you are choosing mediocrity and giving up the true throne of God's abundance, power and authority. Choosing the world is bowing to another kingdom. When a queen bows her head to another kingdom, her crown falls off and her royalty is tarnished. Her strength to rule is submitted to a selfish plight to gain the approval of man.

So can a woman be tenderhearted, filled with God's love, and still rule a kingdom with strength, tenacity, power and excellence? Can a queen wear a crown of humility and grace while still being a strategic negotiator on behalf of Kingdom progress and prosperity? *Yes, she can!* But only by clothing herself with the truth of God's Word and fighting a spiritual battle that knows no gender, no age, no race or background. You are being fit for that battle, even as you continue to read this book. You may not know it, but God is getting you ready, even now, for the greatest victories of your life. You are about to learn what it means to carry the power of heaven on earth and use your female influence to change the world. Queens must not only be seasoned for beauty, but they must equally be seasoned for battle. God not only wants you to be cloaked in grace and honor, but He is about to arm you with truth and justice.

BOOM!—TIME TO REFLECT

Take a moment to do a self-audit. What is the fragrance you bring to a room? Do you bring your garbage to work with you? Do gossip and complaining fill the rooms you enter? Do you take your trash home to share with your family? What can you do, starting today, to carry the scent of heaven and clothe yourself in the fabric of the Kingdom?

Pray this prayer out loud:

Heavenly Father,

I come before You clothed in humility, seeking Your favor. You are the One I adore. You are the One I long to please. I've spent most of my life searching for the "likes" of this world when what I really want is the heart of Your affection. I love You, Lord. I am sorry for carrying the stench of the world into my family, my relationships and even my worship. I ask You to forgive me and cleanse me from all unrighteousness so that I might be a sweet-smelling fragrance for You. In Jesus' name, Amen.

17

An Unlikely Hero

She became known, not because of what was done to her, but what she allowed God to do through her.

For a number of years, I traveled into prisons across America, speaking life and hope into the heart of inmates from all backgrounds. Some were maximum-security prisons, while many were juvenile centers, and still others were women's prisons and rehab or detox facilities. No matter the level of security, a few common denominators were evident at each location. *Brokenness,* abuse and abandonment were the canvas of every story.

While the faces were hardened and their first impressions intimidating, there was always something miraculous about walking through the gated entries and secure passageways, knowing that the God in me could break through any wall in them if the inmates chose to believe. Walking through the gated entries, it was as if I were being taken to a place that others feared crossing. These were murderers, thieves, child molesters, abusers, addicts—individuals often filled with a fury of hatred and mistrust. There was never a facility or location I entered where I did not think to myself, *What am I doing here? And what on earth am I supposed to say that will help bring spiritual freedom to these precious but gravely broken people?*

I always tried to lessen my appearance as a "pretty girl" in fancy clothes living a perfect life. But no matter how average I tried to appear, the jeers and sarcastic scowls would always come when they first saw my appearance. It always caused a moment of intimidation to sweep across my mind, but the Holy Spirit held as strong as scaffolding around me as I continued in my assignment.

But nothing shook me to the core more than the day I walked into a maximum-security prison where the men were chained hand and foot, wearing orange jumpsuits, and having looks of sheer evil painted upon their faces. I was extremely pregnant at the time and thought surely that would settle their usual catcalls and rude remarks. Larry was with me that day, and I had settled in my mind that if my massively protruding belly did not make them be nicer to me, then my six-foot-five, extremely muscular husband would settle them down. But no such luck.

Standing at the back of the room as they ushered the men into the secure area where I would speak, I heard voices permeating my thoughts. *Who do you think you are coming into this place? What could you possibly have to say to these men? They are going to disrespect you and see nothing but the female skin cloaking your tiny spirit.* Then the catcalls started, along with the snide remarks from hecklers. Then, as I stood waiting, I prayed beneath my breath, *God, I am Your servant. If You can use anything, Lord, use me.*

As I was introduced and asked to come to the front of the room, I could see so much brokenness in the inmates' eyes. They looked mean. Their menacing faces looked angry. This was not a church service, and I could tell by the chains on their feet that they were only there by request.

But then something miraculous happened.

Not knowing what to say, I felt the nudge of the Holy Spirit telling me to sing "Amazing Grace." There was no music, no band, no fancy lights, nor a stage of grandeur—just me and the Holy Spirit and a room full of broken hearts. After the first few words flowed from my lips, the atmosphere shifted. God's anointing fell on the rough exteriors of the men and penetrated deep into their hearts as silence filled the room. Soon, heads were bowed and tears fell.

I watched as one man, covered head to toe in wicked-looking tattoos and body markings, began to bawl. Not just a small tear trickling down his face—it was a full-out cry. Shackled hands and feet, when the song was over, he said, "My grandmother used to sing that song. It was her favorite. You messed me up with that!"

God has a way of breaking us down to our most vulnerable state and silencing our ego so He can speak a message of new beginnings into our hearts. My heart was moved as I heard stories of men who, despite their state of imprisonment due to heinous crimes, were still reachable by the Father. And to imagine, through my simple act of saying yes, God could use a country girl like me to be a conduit as He broke through to someone's core.

An Unlikely Choice

Saul of Tarsus, who would later be known as Paul among first-century believers, was much like those hardened criminals. He was not only against the message of Christ, but he sought to capture and slaughter Christians.[1] At that time, Saul would have been the modern-day equivalent of a terrorist or dedicated leader of Isis who would take prisoner, burn or behead anyone who claimed to be of the Christian faith. In addition to his hatred for Christians, Saul also happened to be a very brilliant scholar, business strategist and up-and-coming city official.

"The best and the brightest"—these are the words a journalist once used to describe the administration of President John F. Kennedy.[2] These same words could have been used to describe Saul. A child of the most influential upbringing, Paul was a student of the most credentialed teacher, Gamaliel. Also a Roman citizen, he trained in the finest Jewish schools and was well groomed for success, perhaps even with the great possibility of becoming a chief priest one day. No doubt, Saul was on the fast track to climbing the ladder of notoriety.

In addition to his impressive education, Saul was also trained as an entrepreneur, negotiator and tentmaker. Like other Jewish boys, he was taught a specific trade so it could be a source of financial provision for his future and a way to engage in marketplace influence. Saul learned how to "work with [his] own hands" (1 Corinthians 4:12) as a tentmaker, a skill that would later become his entrepreneurial enterprise and fund his ministry. As Saul grew, so did his intellectual strength and power to negotiate and manipulate others. Because tents were used primarily to provide housing for soldiers, it is likely that the Roman army was one of Saul's most prized customers. Clearly, this was no small operation, and it required that he not only work with his hands but also be a shrewd negotiator and salesman.

As a notable Pharisee and teacher of the law, however, Saul was bankrupt of love and sought to kill and destroy those of the Christian faith. In his hatred toward Christians, he wielded even more power by performing his persecuting work under the direct approval of the highest religious authorities. He used his negotiation skills to ask for official letters from the high priest, authorizing his mission to arrest Christians so they could be persecuted and even killed.

Vexed and Full of Vengeance

Meanwhile, Saul was still breathing out murderous threats against the Lord's disciples. He went to the high priest and asked him for letters to the synagogues in Damascus, so that if he found any there who belonged to the Way, whether men or women, he might take them as prisoners to Jerusalem.

Acts 9:1–2

We do not know exactly how or why Saul became so vexed by the followers of Christ, but what we do know is he was filled with hate and was used as a terrorist to create fear in the minds of believers. No doubt, Saul's ego was enraged by this Galilean known as Jesus of Nazareth. Perhaps he was one of the religious leaders sent to pray for Lazarus before he died and was mortified to see Jesus raise him from the dead. Maybe he was one of the lawyers who convicted Jesus for blasphemy and was outraged when people claimed He had risen from the dead, just as He predicted. Or maybe he was one of the Pharisees in Matthew 23:27, whom Jesus described as hypocrites when He said: "Woe to you, teachers of the law and Pharisees, you hypocrites! You are like whitewashed tombs, which look beautiful on the outside but on the inside are full of the bones of the dead and everything unclean."

No doubt, something or someone, at some point, triggered Saul's ego to the point that he became so outraged and offended that he would give his life to their annihilation. He even approved of the torturous stoning of Stephen, and perhaps that was the beginning of his enlightenment process. Instead of retaliating in hate or threats to hire a lawyer of his own, Stephen simply cried out to God, "Lord, do not charge them with this sin" (Acts 7:60 NKJV).

We do not know how long God was working on Saul or what nightmares he had as a result of such grave sin, but we do know that the Holy Spirit was at work in him while Satan did his best to rule his spirit. After Stephen's plea of forgiveness, Saul became even more fanatical about destroying the growing Christian community and launched a holy war against the Church. But instead of stopping the movement, it scattered the believers and caused the message of Christ to spread even more.

Saul was like a madman hunting Christians, barging into their homes, sending them to prison and advocating their deaths. And all of this commotion was making him a very notable figure in the Roman Empire. When Saul requested permission to go to

Damascus in pursuit of destroying the Christian sect, the high priest granted him letters of authority to take to the synagogues of Syria. Saul was climbing the corporate ladder, and his ego was fueling his aggression.

The thought that this crazy, hate-filled murderer would become the author and writer of most of the New Testament is beyond human understanding, but this is exactly how God works.

Blinded by the Light

"Saul, Saul, why do you persecute me?"

"Who are you, Lord?" Saul asked.

"I am Jesus, whom you are persecuting," he replied. "Now get up and go into the city, and you will be told what you must do."

The men traveling with Saul stood there speechless; they heard the sound but did not see anyone. Saul got up from the ground, but when he opened his eyes he could see nothing. So they led him by the hand into Damascus. For three days he was blind, and did not eat or drink anything.

Acts 9:4–9

God knows exactly what and how to reach even the hardest of criminals and worst of sinners. That is exactly what happened the day God ambushed Saul and his band of haters on the road to Damascus. Their hearts were full of hate when suddenly they were overwhelmed by a glorious flash of light so intense it was like looking directly into the sun on a cloudless day. Saul fell to the ground, and a voice echoed through the light that was both terrifying and full of peace at the same time.

You have to imagine the confusion that flashed through Saul's mind at that moment. I am quite certain this event did not happen as fast as we read about it in a matter of five sentences.

Can you imagine the heart of Saul racing with anger and confusion and love and peace all at the same time? Can you imagine Saul's thoughts when this mysterious voice claimed to be the very One he was hunting down and seeking to eradicate from the earth?

If this really was Jesus, that meant that every Jewish leader in Israel was wrong. It meant that the crucifixion was the murder of an innocent man. It meant Saul, the one who claimed to have lived an impeccable life of obedience to the law, had murdered multitudes of innocent children and families.

Saul's body began to tremble, and when he opened his eyes, he was blind. Even then, the light was so overwhelming, he had to close his eyelids tightly to avoid the intensity. His heart had to have been flooded with a supernatural hunger to obey when he lifted his head and asked, "Lord, what do You want me to do?" (Acts 9:6 NKJV).

Okay, let's stop right here and consider something. This was a pivotal moment in the history of Christianity. Jesus had died only a few years earlier, and the message of His death, burial and resurrection was being snuffed out by the hateful terrorists and anti-Christian spirits of the age.

When Saul stopped and asked, "Lord, what do You want me to do?," Jesus replied, "Arise and go into the city . . ." (Acts 9:6 NKJV). Saul obeyed and was blindly led to a disciple named Ananias, who would become his advocate to the community of believers. When Ananias laid hands on Saul, scales fell from his eyes and he could see again. The only difference was that then, not only could he see in the natural, but he was given supernatural sight to see God's plan for his life (see v. 18). Years later, Saul took on his Roman name, Paul, so that he could better relate to and embrace the Gentiles whom he had been sent to rescue.

Paul was an automatic weapon just waiting to be loaded with God's ammunition. And when God arrested him through a blinding light, it changed everything. Saul of Tarsus went from hater to heretic. His radical shift would become the basis for the writing of nearly one half of the 27 books in the New Testament. Today, Paul is considered one of the most influential people in the history of the world.

Every Knee Will Bow

Now, let's go back to the thought that you might be "underquali-fied" to be a world changer or history maker. If God can use someone like Paul, imagine what He could do with you! Were you ever that diabolical? Have you murdered Christians? Have you been a terrorist of hate and vile darkness? Have you imprisoned innocent children and advocated the rape and destruction of in-nocent lives? Even if you said yes, Paul is proof that you would still be a candidate for God's grace and mercy. God would still be calling on you to be His hands and feet and to spread the message of Christ to the world around you.

For this to become possible, however, the Holy Spirit of God must become real to you, stop you in your tracks and transform you into the image of God. That same Holy Spirit arrested Paul and changed eternity in the flash of a light.

When Saul said, "Lord, what do You want me to do?," he was echoing Noah's faith to build an ark,[3] Abraham's faith to raise the knife to his son,[4] Mary's faith to offer her womb[5] and even Jesus' faith to declare to His Father, "Not my will, but yours be done."[6]

If you have ever thought that our world has gone to hell in a handbasket, think about this moment in time when God steps in and says, *Let Me show you how I can shift the world in one mo-ment or one flash of light.*

No matter where you are in this moment, *stop* and ask this question: *Master, what do You want me to do?*

I assure you, this moment will be like none other you have ever experienced. In this moment, if you truly seek His face and hunger to hear His voice, you *will* hear God. Take this moment and allow Him to reveal how He wants you to use your life, your talents, your passions, your past and even your failures to spread the Good News of Jesus Christ to the world around you.

Maybe it is difficult to see yourself as a powerhouse leader in the marketplace or a voice of truth to your generation. Perhaps you have thought, *I don't have any special talents and even if He wanted to, why would God use me? I've made so many mistakes, my past is certainly not spotless, and I am not qualified to lead in business or ministry.* These are words that I once said to myself after experiencing a devastating relationship breakup at the age of 23 that yielded suicidal depression and a worthless and abused mindset. But the truth is that brokenness sets a heart up for humility and service that can fuel great leadership and compassion for others.

God does not look for perfect vessels. He searches for willing vessels and warriors with a passion and hunger to make a difference in the world. In EMwomen, we rescue women and girls who have survived some of the most horrible traumas and stories of abuse. At face value, many of them feel worthless, unwanted, abused, dirty and even ashamed. But the statement we say at every meeting is one I mentioned earlier:

Every woman has a story, and every
story can change the world.

God searches the earth looking for someone in whom He can prove Himself strong. He searches for passion, hunger and a willingness to be radically used for a purpose greater than oneself. That is exactly what He did when He seized the attention of Saul of Tarsus, one of the most wretched anti-Christian leaders in history.

BOOM!—TIME TO REFLECT

As we continue our journey into equipping you for marketplace ministry, ask yourself these questions:

1. Am I passionate about making a difference in the world?
2. Am I in a job, position or vocation that can bring honor to God?

3. Am I willing to sharpen my skills so my talents can make way for me in the marketplace?

4. Am I willing to say yes to allowing God to use me to advance the Kingdom of God?

5. Am I willing to give up my pride so that God can use me to bring hope, help and healing to others?

If you said yes to any of the above questions, *you* are qualified to be the hands and feet of Jesus to the marketplace. God does not look at pedigrees. He searches for humility and availability. When you say yes, the molding process of your spirit truly begins. Pray this prayer out loud:

God,

This is me saying yes to Your will. I don't fully know how, when or what it is You want to do with my life, but what I know for certain is that I surrender to Your plan. If You can use anything, Lord, please use me. Mold me, shape me, re-create me if You must, but please, Father, let my life be an extension of Your passion and mercy for this generation. In Jesus' name, Amen.

18

Conduits of His Spirit

Let her sleep, for when she wakes up, she will move mountains!

I t is snowing outside as I write this portion of the book. What a joy that the snow fell today, on the weekend dedicated to shutting myself away to be in the presence of the Holy Spirit and write more pages. The snow fell after a beautiful week of seventy-degree weather. All week long, I used the perfect weather to work diligently in getting my family moved into a new town-home in Frisco, Texas. We downsized from a large home to be less about our personal lifestyle and more about His Kingdom.

When we decided to say yes to an intentional decrease, my nineteen-year-old son, Payton, asked if he could also make a shift of seasons and get an apartment with his real estate partner and start a new chapter of entrepreneurial independence in downtown Dallas. People have always told me it would be difficult when the day your firstborn leaves the nest, but after years of pouring the love and wisdom of Christ into him and watching his own journey of being fueled by fire and empowered by the Holy Spirit, we knew it was God's will and we fully supported his decision.

As he moved out, we found ourselves being stripped of beds, TVs, stools and anything else two bachelors might need in their new adventure.

At first, seeing the many items he wanted, I felt something in my flesh say, *He's taking advantage of you.* I could hear voices saying, *Are you just going to let him take everything you've got? You have to have those stools for your townhome. You will need those lamps in your own living room. He isn't even grateful, and that TV is expensive.* Suddenly, I started to feel frustration settling in my flesh. I started to say something, but paused and listened to the Holy Spirit for a moment.

In that pause, I could sense the Holy Spirit say, *Let it go. I will bless you for blessing his faithfulness in this season. You are writing this chapter of his life, so make it a chapter he will never forget. Seal it with prayer and anoint the doors of his new apartment with oil so that he never forgets the covenant I have with him in that place.*

So, my son and his buddy received beds, chairs, stools, pictures, towels, pillows, dishes, silverware, Crock-Pots and anything else they needed. I thought many times, *Okay, enough is enough!* But the Holy Spirit kept saying, *Let it go!* As we moved the items into his new apartment, we finished with a beautiful time of prayer and worship.

His friends—some are Christians, and some are "searching"— gathered with us as we anointed every window and door with oil and declared it as holy ground for Kingdom purposes. We wanted them all to know that our son is marked for Kingdom authority and they should all become watchmen of the anointing that rests upon his life.

As we left, I thought, *Oh, dear me, now I need new towels, stools and stuff to go into our townhome.* Little did I know that the Holy Spirit was not only setting me up for some great bargains, but that there would be salespeople in the process who would need prayer, deliverance and healing. The Holy Spirit was not just blessing my son—He was positioning me in the marketplace to pray for hurting people.

One of my dearest friends, who has watched the Holy Spirit flow through these moments of my life for over a decade, came to town, and together we took action.

First, we stopped at IHOP for breakfast, where our waitress, Lisa, became our first target. She cried and cried as we prayed for her and her sick aunt. Then came Jason, the salesman at the TV clearance center at Nebraska Furniture. After he wrote up our ticket, I said, "Hey, Jason, I pray for people and run a ministry of healing and deliverance. Is there anything we can pray with you about before we leave?" Again, a portal of heaven opened upon that young man as we prayed, and the Holy Spirit broke him into tears as he shared some of his current family needs.

Next came the Dish Network man, the fireplace repairman, the two TV installation guys, the bar stool salesman and Shaila, a young lady who had been badly abused by her boyfriend. Over the course of five short days of bargain shopping and moving, we prayed for numerous people to receive healing, wisdom and financial breakthrough. We even introduced one of them to the Lord for the first time.

Our shopping trips became a revival. Every salesperson and every laborer who came to our home received the fire of God through prayer in a matter of a few short days. When I hear people say, "O God, send us revival. O God, let Your fire pour!" I want to stand up and shout, "Revival has *already come*! His name is Jesus, and His Holy Spirit is a fire that burns daily through us. *We* are the revival, and the Holy Spirit is the fire!"

The Disease of "Me"

God wants to demonstrate His power on earth by using ordinary, broken and battered vessels as conduits of His miracles on earth.

So many times, we get down on ourselves, thinking, *I'm not good enough. I'm not smart enough. I don't have a big enough social following. I'm too poor, too white, too black, too fat, too skinny, or too uneducated.* But the truth is, it is not about you. When we put ourselves and our lack of abilities before a total trust in God, we are succumbing to the disease of "me."

This is the great mystery that so many people have forgotten or simply chosen to disregard. We are *not* the source of power. Our talents are *not* the source of God's ability to shift nations. Our jobs, titles and even our families are *not* the sources of the significance God wants to have through us. Instead, it is the Holy Spirit who lives in us, as Christians, to empower us to do great exploits and reflect His glory to those around us.

Just look throughout Scripture and you will see that God uses the foolish things of this world to confound the wise. He chooses harlots, tax collectors, cowards, fishermen, doctors, stonemasons and even little girls like Mary to birth His miracles throughout history.

You can spend your entire life striving for success but never find real and lasting significance. Why? Because you may be too consumed trying to fit into the world's standards instead of surrendering to God's standards and saying, *If You can use anything, Lord, use me!*

Jesus told His disciples, "Most assuredly, I say to you, he who believes in Me, the works that I do he will do also; and greater works than these he will do, because I go to My Father. And whatever you ask in My name, that I will do" (John 14:12 NKJV).

God wants to flow His miracle-working power through you. God wants to use your voice and your brazen boldness to change policies, stand against injustice and perhaps even shift governments. The talents and passions that you were given are not about *you*. They are about *Him* using you as a vessel so that *He* will be glorified on earth. The marketplace around you is your mission field. Your job or talent is the platform you will use to communicate *new life* to the world around you.

200

Nothing will bring you more peace than knowing you are being used by the God of the universe as a vessel who brings heaven to earth. Something marvelous takes place in your emotions when you know you are tapped into your divine purpose and aligned with the Source of all creation. The more you let God's light shine through you, the more you will see that *you* are an asset to the Kingdom of God. He will use your story and your testimony to connect with other hurting people and start a revival of hope and healing all around you. You do not have to be broken, bitter or fearful anymore. You can awaken to your divine purpose and let the Holy Spirit of God turn your trials into a testimony and your frustrations into fuel that makes Him known wherever you go.

Becoming a Force of Change

The definition of *revival* is to bring back to life that which is dead. To revive something means to awaken the consciousness back to its original purpose. It is the restoration of force that rests behind a contract.

My friend, we are God's agents of revival, and it is up to us to bring back to life the souls of those who are dead in sin and turn their consciousness toward a new life in Christ. That is the contract of revival. It is a new covenant of hope, and it is our mandate on earth.

We are not waiting on God for revival. God is waiting on us to rise up with the power of the Holy Spirit and move mountains on behalf of others. Do not sit around "waiting for a move of God." Be the move of God someone else is praying for today. Be bold, be confident in His power and be courageous in setting a fire of revival in the hearts of others. You were placed on this planet to do more than perform a talent. You are here to reflect the one and true living God and to become a vessel that displays His glory to those around you.

God has a strategic plan for your life, your successes, your brokenness and even your past traumas. Unfortunately, all too often, I hear women struggling to identify what their purpose in life might be. *Who am I? Why am I here*, they may ask. Many try to find fulfillment through their job, talents, kids or their family, assuming those things are their purpose and what deserves their greatest attention. But if something disrupts one of those areas of focus, they end up devastated and somehow believing that their purpose in life must change.

But expressing your talents, gaining a mass following or raising a family are *not* your divine purpose. It is not your job, your marriage, your abilities, nor is it the organizations you may serve or create. They are tools that support your purpose or give it a place to shine, but they are not why God placed you on this planet. So what is it? Why did God put you, me and every human being on this earth? *To know Him and the power of His resurrection and to make Him known in all the earth.*

BOOM!—there it is. You have found it. No matter what job you choose to take or talent you choose to express, God's purpose for you is to use that job, talent or shopping spree to reflect the light and love of God everywhere you go. You can go ahead and save yourself hundreds or even thousands of dollars in searching through books, motivational seminars or online courses to discover your purpose.

Knowing God and becoming a conduit of His Spirit on earth is why you are here. It is your purpose, and it should be your highest pursuit in life. If you fulfill that mission, you will shine like a diamond through your talents, you will shake nations, you will reflect God's power to your children and family, at the hospital, at work, in the grocery store and anywhere you happen to be placed at any given moment. Suddenly you will see a car accident not as an inconvenience but as a potential opportunity to share the love of God with others caught in the circumstance with you. You will see a long line at the grocery store not as a frustration but as a delay that may be positioning you by others to let your light shine.

> "You're here to be light, bringing out the God-colors in the world. God is not a secret to be kept. We're going public with this, as public as a city on a hill. If I make you light-bearers, you don't think I'm going to hide you under a bucket, do you? I'm putting you on a light stand. Now that I've put you there on a hilltop, on a light stand—shine!"
>
> Matthew 5:14–16 MSG

When you know God's purpose for your life, you will see life on earth differently. Every circumstance, setback, plumbing issue, flat tire or shopping experience becomes a way for you to connect God's love with people you otherwise would not see. Simply put, you are here to reflect the glory of God and shine forth His brilliant love to the world around you.

BOOM!—TIME TO REFLECT

When you go through your day, do you see the multiple ways God wants to use you to touch the lives of those around you? When you get a cold and need a doctor, do you simply go to the clinic and get what you need, or do you see it as an opportunity to take the love of God to that clinic and be a source of hope to someone in your pathway? When you get delayed in a long line at the grocery store, do you grow frustrated, or do you use the time to engage in a compassionate conversation with the people around you? There are no accidents when you are in service to God. He can take every setback and use it as a setup for you to reach someone in need. What is a common excuse you may have used in the past that keeps you from sharing your faith with others?

What can you do this week to be a more courageous woman of God in your everyday life?

Pray this prayer out loud:

God,

I am so sorry for being mostly concerned about my own time, my own life, my own health and even my own passions. I can see that nothing can get to me that You don't want to use to get through me to other people, including colds, traffic, school lines, funerals and anything that might cause me frustrations or momentary suffering. Help me see when You are using life's circumstances to move into the lives of those around me. I want to be Your conduit of love to the world around me, and I'm asking You, now, to give me ears to hear and eyes to see what You see. In Jesus' name I pray, Amen.

19

Don't Retreat—Reload!

She might be broken, bruised, and a tad bit weary, but never underestimate the power of a woman under the influence of the Holy Spirit.

Have you ever had someone come against you with such emotional force that it knocks the wind out of you? Perhaps you have felt the feeling of someone in authority holding you back or a co-worker who gets under your skin. Do you know what it feels like to have continual opposition trying to get that "big deal" signed and closed? Or what about the times when you and your spouse hit an impasse, and though you have tried to come to an agreement with words, flowers, kind gestures or creative antics, you just cannot seem to repair the canyon of separation between you? These are just a few examples of spiritual battles that require a spiritual response. These are not flesh wars—they are spirit wars.

I will never forget a time when I was involved in a huge clash of personalities with another executive leader in one of the companies where I was working. This leader was determined to be at odds with me, no matter what I did to tolerate and appease him. I had no real proof of this man's motives, but I just knew something was not right in our relationship, and it seemed there was a spiritual force of darkness all around him.

"I think this guy is totally set on sabotaging me and my efforts," I confided to my husband.

I continued to ask for God's wisdom and breakthrough against any principalities and powers of darkness who would try to stop me from doing what God had called me to do for that company. Then one day, I called the office and asked to speak with him about a client I was working with. He was bullish and demeaning in his tone with me.

Dear God, help me with this guy, I prayed, *and give me patience not to say something I will regret later!*

When he hung up the phone, he accidentally pushed the speaker button instead of ending the call, which allowed me to hear into the room. He proceeded to speak harshly about me to someone in his office, using foul names and hatred like I had never heard before.

I sat on the other end of the phone, dumbfounded. After listening for a good thirty seconds, everything inside of me wanted to scream. But the Holy Spirit said, *Be gentle. Be broken. Let him know you are listening.*

"Uhh . . . Bill," I said gently, "I'm still here on the phone."

Silence.

I could imagine the look on his face, as well as his blood pressure that was probably skyrocketing at that moment. Instantly, I knew I had him in "checkmate," and my guardian angels had shifted the spiritual environment on my behalf.

I continued, "I'm so sorry to hear these words from you and even more sorry for the implication this means to our company."

Come to find out, this was not the first or even the worst situation that the company had encountered with him. A short time later, he was fired from his position, and God used my calm demeanor in the situation to create favor and respect in a way I could have never set up in the natural realm.

This story is a great example of how principalities can be released in a company and stagnate growth due to internal conflict. Had I fought only with words or anger, I would have never seen progress. But when we realize that our battle is not against people "but against principalities" (Ephesians 6:12 KJV), we can fight fire with the fire of love, gentleness and profound wisdom in the moment—what Paul called "the *good* fight for the true faith" (1 Timothy 6:11–12 NLT, emphasis added).

This applies to marriages, friendships, corporate contracts and even negotiations. *Make sure you are fighting a good fight of faith and not a battle of words.* When we sense that there is a force set against us or the alignments we are called to unify, we should never look at the person across from us and engage in a fleshly battle. Instead, look up and recognize that this is a battle we must fight in the Spirit. If we try to win the battle with words, we will set ourselves back and potentially destroy the relationship. Instead, we wage war in the Spirit and pray for wisdom that allows God to shift the outcome in our favor.

Heaven's Firepower

"In solemn truth I tell you, anyone believing in me shall do the same miracles I have done, and even greater ones, because I am going to be with the Father."

John 14:12 TLB

God came to earth in the form of man (Jesus) to serve as a living example of how to wage war in the marketplace and take spiritual dominion over principalities, demons, sickness, disease and temptations of every kind. He did not come to write a book about motivational tips for financial increase or to give inspirational tips on how to achieve your business goals. While these seem to be popular pulpit messages, Jesus came from heaven to earth to teach us how to carry the fire of God's Spirit, win souls, heal the sick, conquer death, annihilate forces of darkness and set free those who live in bondage. This was not the popular message of Jesus' day, nor will it be the popular message that sells the most books today. But it is *the* message that is most desperately needed, and now is the time to be unafraid to share it with the masses.

Following that inaugural public miracle of turning the water into wine, Jesus became a living example of heaven on earth. He used miracles, signs and wonders to demonstrate the Kingdom of God on earth as it is in heaven. His display of victory over sin and darkness was not so that people would merely say, "Wow!" But His radical faith and example was to make us say, "Wow, if He can do it, I can do it!"

Jesus used every minute of every day to teach His disciples how to wage war in a realm not of this world. He taught them about the Kingdom of God and how to gain territory over sin and darkness. He was not trying to fit into the culture that captured the popular opinion. Instead, He was creating a counter-culture that established His Father's business on earth as it is in heaven. This is how we should be "modeling" our faith to our children and families today. Instead of simply saying, "Do as Jesus did," we must lead by example saying, "Do as I do. Follow me as I follow Christ." Our world needs more role models of what it means to be fueled by fire and empowered by the truth of God's Word.

The disciples had a hard time fully grasping what Jesus was trying to tell them when He said, "What I am doing now, you will do even greater once I return to the right hand of God in heaven" (see John 14:12). Jesus was showing them that a massive shift was about to take place where the fire of His Spirit would soon flood their lives, and they, too, would become the primary conduits for miracles on earth.

"I tell you, it is for your good that I am going away. Unless I go away, the Advocate [the Holy Spirit] will not come to you; but if I go, I will send him to you. When he comes, he will prove the world to be in the wrong about sin and righteousness and judgment. . . . I have much more to say to you, more than you can now bear. But when he, the Spirit of truth, comes, he will guide you into all the truth."

John 16:7–13

From that point forward, Jesus shifted His ministry from being a "watch and learn" experience into a Spirit-empowered "Go, show and tell" ministry. Upon sending the Holy Spirit, He transferred authority to anyone who believes, including you and me.

"Go into all the world and preach the gospel to all creation. Whoever believes and is baptized will be saved, but whoever does not believe will be condemned. And these signs will accompany those who believe: In my name they will drive out demons; they will speak in new tongues; they will pick up snakes with their hands; and when they drink deadly poison, it will not hurt them at all; they will place their hands on sick people, and they will get well."

Mark 16:15–18

What does that mean for you? It means that when you are filled with the fire of God's Spirit, you will do what Jesus did and become a portal of heaven to earth. You will love your enemies but also bring clarity of truth. You will forgive those who have persecuted you, sacrifice your selfish motives for the greater good and wage war in the Spirit so that justice for all will be served. The more you do what Jesus did, the less you will be loved and coddled by the masses. Your brazen faith will no doubt attract opposition, persecution, isolation and spiritual warfare as you bring truth and justice to the world around you. A counterattack against you will be orchestrated by principalities and powers of darkness.

209

Satan does not want you to embrace this firepower. He would rather you stay locked in a life of mediocrity. He wants you trapped within your comfort zone. He will try every tactic in his book to hinder and even stop you from being an effective witness of influence at work, at home and in the marketplace. He will put people in your pathway to frustrate you, accuse you, tempt you and even confuse you into submission to his lies.

To fight with heaven's firepower means you fight with your gloves off. Instead of throwing punches, you throw love. Instead of wielding human weapons, you fight with the sword of God's Word and the fruit of God's Spirit.

Fight Fire with Fire

The world we live in appears to be controlled by irrational human opinions, financially fortified corporations and public personalities with a high level of social influence. It seems, in the natural, that the power of the elites or the popular vote of the masses rules the lives of people on earth. While all these things and people of positional power reflect what earth has made a priority, they are simply *not* what controls the universe. The marketplace—including schools, companies, governments, sports franchises and even some churches—is under the power of principalities and spiritual forces. While human faces and corporate brands are what stands at the foreground of our boardrooms, courtrooms and classrooms, they are mere puppets on a string to the spirits to which they have yielded their power. The battle we face is in the heavenly realm, and only through the power of God's Spirit will we truly be able to take dominion over darkness in the marketplace.

"For our struggle is not against flesh and blood, but against the rulers, against the authorities, against the powers of this dark world and against the spiritual forces of evil in the heavenly realms" (Ephesians 6:10).

I cannot repeat this Scripture enough and I encourage you to memorize it, meditate on it, know it and let it sink deep into your spirit. This is the key to unlock the door to decoding the crazy relationships in your life that can sometimes drive you cray-cray! Stop for just a moment and read that Scripture *at least* three times. Memorize it if you can. It is the secret sauce to creating a life and business you love. It is the treasure map for power. It reveals where your greatest attention should be set and where you should spend the majority of your focus.

When you are having struggles or frustrations with people in your life, do not be deceived. It is not a battle of human flesh. You are engaging in spiritual warfare. To try to fix broken people or situations in the natural would be like boxing the wind. It will not get you victory. You have to connect in full force with your real enemy, which are the spiritual influences standing behind or in front of those people who seem to be driving you up the wall.

It is impossible to win a spiritual war without being filled with the fire of God's Spirit. There are conversations, ideas, strategies and thoughts that are foolishness to the human mind. Instead, they can only be discerned by the Spirit of God living in us. "For who among men knows the thoughts of a man except the spirit of the man which is in him? Even so the thoughts of God no one knows except the Spirit of God" (1 Corinthians 2:11 NASB).

You must have fire to win.

Never mess with a woman who has put on her spiritual combat boots and is ready to take back what the enemy has tried to steal in her life. She might have lost a few battles, but when a woman, on fire with the Holy Spirit, truly awakens, she will storm the gates of hell with passion, purpose and unlimited potential. God is raising up an army of this type of woman, and hell's demons are panicking because they know the fury of a woman scorned and the damage to darkness her sword can yield. The spiritual assault on women today and the deceptive lies being displayed 24/7 are a sign that Satan knows his time is short. He knows that women will play a critical role in the preparation of the Bride of Christ prior to Jesus' return. Just as a woman birthed the Savior into the world, so will women be catalysts in preparing the Bride for the Bridegroom to return.

3-2-1 BOOM!

The day I fully surrendered to God was a day like no other. I sat down with a pen and paper and felt the Father saying,

Staci, will you be a yielded vessel in My hands? Will you be one that I can shape and mold into My image and one that I can flow through freely to the world around you? Be holy as I am holy. This will not be an easy task, as many will try to convince you that in order to be a success, you must blend into the world's standards. But I tell you, "The purer the vessel, the greater the flow of My power."

I will give you peace and power that the world has never known. But first, there is much cleaning to do in you, and you will need to go through a season of great surrender and purification before you will be fully ready for what I have called you to do. The desires of your flesh must be overcome by the power of My Spirit. The purer the vessel, the greater the flow of My power.

Remove all distractions and weights that would hinder you from fulfilling what I am asking you to do. Focus your eyes on Me and Me alone. Don't try to figure things out. I will handle the details and direct your steps. Just focus on becoming a willing and purified vessel and see what I can do.

That was the day when the Holy Spirit became alive to me and became my best friend in this journey called life. On that day, I chose no longer to be fueled by my ego or my lust for the things of this world. Instead, I became fueled by the fire of God. I began to say *yes* to helping the elderly lady get her packages to her car. I said *yes* to asking the waitress if I could pray for her. I said *yes* to the homeless man who asked for food by giving him a granola bar and prayer. I said *yes* to walking away from what pleased me and stepping into a life that was pleasing to the Father. The more I said yes, the more I saw signs, wonders and miracles appear. With every yes came greater authority and confidence in God's miracle-working power. Soon, God made bigger asks that required ridiculous faith.

Today, being fueled by fire means knowing, with a certainty that outweighs all certainty, that I am not looking for a move of God—*I am a move of God*. And His Spirit, in me, is looking for lives to touch, hearts to heal and homes to restore. As my dear friend Nicole Binion sings so eloquently in "Living Proof," we are living proof that God is on the move. Faith will rise up when we realize He has saved us and freed us. There is nothing our God cannot do.[1]

That is my prayer for you. I pray that you begin to see that the fiery furnace of this world does not have to destroy you. Instead, you can be fueled by the fire of God and live, fully empowered, to be the hands and feet of Jesus everywhere you go to everyone you meet.

Go into all the world and share the Good News to everyone everywhere.

This is our mandate as women of God and queens called to carry the fragrance of heaven to the world around us. No matter what season you are in, *now* is the time to buckle up your belt of truth, pull out the sword of the Spirit, embrace the breastplate of righteousness, and while you are at it, go ahead and strap on your cape. The army of Warrior Queens that God is assembling today is going to storm the gates of hell, take back what the enemy stole, boldly fight for our families and be the love the world so desperately needs today. It is time to prepare for the greatest victory of your lifetime. You are destined for greatness, and your *best* days begin now.

Stop for a moment and ask the Holy Spirit to open your ears to hear this chapter clearly. The enemy does not want you to keep reading this book. He does not want you to grasp the magnitude of the power you possess when you are fueled by the fire of God's Spirit. The strategy of warfare you have learned will give you supernatural wisdom in how to govern your family affairs, rule your emotions, fortify your marriage, shift kingdoms, silence the enemy and rescue the people God has placed in your pathway. For those of you who carry a Joan of Arc spirit, get ready to put on your armor to fully protect you in your quest to gain Kingdom territory on behalf of truth and justice.

You might have been knocked down and be walking with a limp from the battles you have faced, but take a moment and regroup, my dear friend, because warriors don't retreat—*they reload*. Your mess has been a setup for the message you are about to carry. The story of your past is about to meet the destiny of your future. Your spiritual womb, when touched by the fire of God, will set ablaze a revolution that impacts the lives of everyone around you. Are you ready?

It is simple. Say, "3-2-1 BOOM!"

Say it again: "3-2-1 BOOM!"

Now, this time, shift your physiology. Stand up. Turn around. Walk outside. Scream if you must, but do something that shifts your posture out of a mediocre mindset when you say, "3-2-1 BOOM!"

Let's go! It is time for war. Now is the time, this is the place, and *you* are the one who will start a revolution.

BOOM!—TIME TO REFLECT

Can you think of a time when you knew there were forces fighting against you, your family or your business? Perhaps you mistakenly thought that the issue was your husband, your co-worker or another human being. But in reality, the war is not on a human level. It is a spiritual battle to keep you, as a queen in God's arsenal, from being the force of light and power He has destined you to be. Imagine you are the queen on God's chessboard. It is your move. What can you do, starting right now, to shift the game in His favor? What simple act of faith can you do right now that will add more love, patience, kindness, forgiveness or mercy to the circumstances of your life?

Pray this prayer aloud:

God,

I am Your queen, and I am ready to make the necessary moves to help You win this war over evil. I trust You to guide me, direct me, mold me and shape me into the courageous woman and warrior You need me to be for my family, my peers and my nation. Fill me with the firepower of Your Spirit and teach me to be more like You. I am a warrior of light, and I refuse the temptation to retreat. Instead, reload me with Your Word. Ignite a fire within me to make the moves that change the world around me. In Jesus' name, Amen.

Acknowledgments

To my precious husband, you are simply the most amazing life partner God could have ever assigned to my life. Thank you for celebrating what God continues to do in our lives and the amazing miracles we are so blessed to experience in His service.

Payton and Alexia, my dear children, your lives continue to be an anvil that God uses to help shape me into a better leader, listener, see-er and servant of God. Thank you for letting me come to you, challenge you, guide you and love you with eyes and ears that were deeply in tune with the Holy Spirit. I know you thought I had eyes in the back of my head sometimes, but truly, it was the eyes of the Spirit guiding me at times when He wanted to protect you most.

Terry and Donna Toler, had you not introduced me to our dear friend Bruce Barbour, this book would not exist. Your pursuit of touching people's lives through the written word and, Bruce, your life of dedication to this craft have paved the way for countless women to be inspired to live a life on fire by the Holy Spirit. Thank you for your friendship, partnership and trust.

To all of my precious EMwomen (Empowered Women), you are the "why" to this book. Having watched each of you transform from extreme brokenness and abuse into women of power and might is what gave me the courage to know that this message can restore, heal and cause radical metamorphosis in the life of any woman, from any background, with any scars, into a powerful source of light and the miracle-working power of God.

To my precious mother, Daddy would be so proud to see you standing strong, empowering nations, shifting mindsets and being a guiding light to your family and friends. Thank you for always challenging me to be relentless in my pursuit of the Father. Your example continues to inspire me, and I will live forever grateful.

Thank you, Kim Bangs and the team at Chosen Books, for hearing the Father's heart in our conversations so much that you would want to swing the bat for this message. Thank you, Christy Callahan, Elisa Tally and Jane Campbell. Although I have not met you in person, we have been so united by the Spirit through this process. Thank you for reminding me of my assignment to be a clarifying voice to women and a living example of what it means to be fully inflamed by the Holy Spirit to do, see, be and live with eyes wide open.

And certainly, thank You, Lord. You are the topic, character and voice of this book. It is You whom I most adore and most seek to please. Thank You for choosing me to write a small piece of the ongoing miracles You continue to manifest on earth. I look forward to many more chapters of many more books that tell of your miracle-working power. To You I give all the glory, all the praise and all the honor.

Notes

Introduction: B.O.O.M. (Breaking Out of Mediocrity)

1. Nancy Hall, ed., "Mach Number," NASA, https://www.grc.nasa.gov/www /k-12/airplane/mach.html.

Part One: Unleashing Your Inner Superhero

1. *Merriam-Webster.com Dictionary*, s.v. "unleash," https://www.merriam -webster.com/dictionary/unleash.

Chapter 1: Satan's Kryptonite

1. *Merriam-Webster.com Dictionary*, s.v. "agreement," https://www.merriam -webster.com/dictionary/agreement.

Chapter 2: Warriors in Training

1. See 2 Timothy 1:7.
2. See Philippians 4:13.

Chapter 5: Mindset Reset

1. 1 Kings 19:12; 1 Samuel 15:22.

Part Two: From Broken to Brazen

1. *Merriam-Webster.com Dictionary*, s.v. "brazen," https://www.merriam -webster.com/dictionary/brazen.

Chapter 6: Satan's Worst Nightmare

1. "G5045—tektōn," *Strong's Greek Lexicon* (KJV), Blue Letter Bible, https:// www.blueletterbible.org//lang/lexicon/lexicon.cfm?Strongs=g5045&t=kjv.

2. Robby Gallaty, "Was Jesus a Carpenter or a Stonemason?" CP Opinion, April 29, 2017, https://www.christianpost.com/news/jesus-carpenter-or-stone mason.html.

3. Muhtar Kent, chairman of the board and CEO, The Coca-Cola Company, October 2010, quoted in "Fast Facts: Marketing to Women," M2W Conference, https://m2w.biz/fast-facts/.

4. "Inspired Investing: Helping Women Achieve Financial Stature," Bloomberg Live, March 8, 2019, https://www.bloomberglive.com/inspired-investing-helping -women-achieve-financial-stature/.

5. Andrea Learned, *Don't Think Pink: What Really Makes Women Buy—and How to Increase Your Share of This Crucial Market*, 1st ed. (Amacom, 2004).

6. "Women at Work," U.S. Bureau of Labor Statistics, March 2017, https:// www.bls.gov/spotlight/2017/women-at-work/.

7. TNS Global, quoted in "Fast Facts: Marketing to Moms," M2M Conference, https://www.m2moms.com/fast-facts/.

8. Claire Behar, quoted in Stephanie Holland, "Marketing to Women Quick Facts," She-conomy, http://she-conomy.com/report/marketing-to-women-quick-facts.

9. American Enterprise Institute, quoted in "Fast Facts: Marketing to Women," M2W Conference, https://m2w.biz/fast-facts/.

10. "Employment Characteristics of Families Summary," Economic News Release, U.S. Bureau of Labor Statistics, April 21, 2020, https://www.bls.gov /news.release/famee.nr0.htm.

Chapter 7: Fearless and Courageous

1. Quoted in Mark Siebert, *The Franchisee Handbook* (Entrepreneur Press: 2019), Kindle edition, emphasis added.

2. American Express, *The 2017 State of Women-Owned Businesses Report*, http://about.americanexpress.com/news/docs/2017-state-of-women-owned-bus inesses-report.pdf, 3.

3. *State of Women-Owned Businesses Report*, 3.

4. Josie Green, "Who Invented the Dishwasher, Windshield Wiper, Caller ID? Women Created These 50 Inventions," *USA Today*, March 16, 2019, https://www .usatoday.com/story/money/2019/03/16/inventions-you-have-women-inventors -thank-these-50-things/39158677/.

5. "Spanx Startup Story," Fundable, https://www.fundable.com/learn/start up-stories/spanx.

Chapter 8: Claiming Your Inheritance

1. See Luke 16:10.

Chapter 9: Anointed for Battle

1. *Merriam-Webster.com Dictionary*, s.v. "anoint," https://www.merriam -webster.com/dictionary/anoint.

2. Jesus said, "The thief comes only to steal and kill and destroy; I have come that they may have life, and have it to the full" (John 10:10).

3. Siebert, *The Franchisee Handbook.*

4. Caroline Leaf, *Think, Learn, Succeed* (Grand Rapids: Baker, 2018), Ebook edition.

5. Leaf, *Think, Learn, Succeed.*

6. "Stacking" is a reference I have used for decades in my coaching of corporate executives and even women who have been molested, raped or abused. The stacking principle is not something I read in a book but a method I have seen by which people grasp a mental understanding of what happens when emotions are not sifted and released from the human body. See also *Atomic Habits* (Avery, 2018), James Clear's fabulous book that talks about the value of habits over goals and tells the reader how to create new daily habits and let them "stack" so they create new progress and behaviors.

7. "Charles R. Swindoll Quotes," Goodreads, https://www.goodreads.com /author/quotes/5139.Charles_R_Swindoll.

Part Three: Armed and Dangerous

1. *Merriam-Webster.com Dictionary*, s.v. "armor," https://www.merriam -webster.com/dictionary/armor.

Chapter 10: Buckle Up Tight, Warrior Queen: The Belt of Truth

1. *A Dictionary of Greek and Roman Antiquities*, "Cin´gulum," William Smith, William Wayte, G. E. Marindin, eds. (Albemarle Street, London: John Murray, 1890), http://www.perseus.tufts.edu/hopper/text?doc=Perseus:text:19 99.04.0063:id=cingulum-cn.

2. Ephesians 6:14 NASB. See also 1 Peter 1:13 KJV: "Wherefore gird up the loins of your mind, be sober, and hope to the end for the grace that is to be brought unto you at the revelation of Jesus Christ."

Chapter 11: Guard Your Heart above All: The Breastplate of Righteousness

1. Encyclopaedia Britannica Editors, "Cuirass," *Encyclopædia Britannica*, March 16, 2016, https://www.britannica.com/technology/cuirass.

2. See Ephesians 6:12; John 10:10.

3. "The Top 10 Causes of Death," World Health Organization, May 24, 2018, https://www.who.int/news-room/fact-sheets/detail/the-top-10-causes-of-death.

4. Luke 4:4, 8–9; Matthew 4:4, 6, 10.

5. Matthew 25:21, 23 NLT.

6. See Ezekiel 28:12–19.

Chapter 12: Put On Your Supernatural Nikes: The Shoes of the Gospel of Peace

1. History.com editors, "Battle of Marathon," *History*, October 8, 2019, https://www.history.com/topics/ancient-history/battle-of-marathon; http: //www.findingdulcinea.com/news/sports/2010/april/Myth-of-Pheidippides-and -the-Marathon.html.

2. Denis Cummings, "The Myth of Pheidippides and the Marathon," Finding Dulcinea, November 04, 2011, http://www.findingdulcinea.com/news/sports/20 10/april/Myth-of-Pheidippides-and-the-Marathon.html.

3. "Readiness," UK Dictionary, Lexico.com, https://www.lexico.com/defi nition/readiness.

4. Saugat Adhikari, "Top 10 Ancient Roman Armor and Costume," Ancient History Lists, April 29, 2019, https://www.ancienthistorylists.com/rome-history /top-10-ancient-roman-armor-and-costume/.

Chapter 13: Quench the Enemy's Fiery Darts: The Shield of Faith

1. Jon Guttman, "Roman Gladius and Scutum: Carving Out an Empire," HistoryNet, https://www.historynet.com/roman-gladius-and-scutum-carving -out-an-empire.htm.

2. Guttman, "Roman Gladius and Scutum."

3. *Merriam-Webster.com Dictionary*, s.v. "substance," https://www.merriam -webster.com/dictionary/substance.

4. *Merriam-Webster.com Dictionary*, s.v. "evidence," https://www.merriam -webster.com/dictionary/evidence.

5. Amritham Viveka, "Amritham Viveka, The Shoe Story," Inspiring Stories, October 3, 2012, http://amritham99.blogspot.com/2012/10/the-shoe-story .html.

6. George Bernard Shaw, *Back to Methuselah*, act I, *Selected Plays with Prefaces*, vol. 2, p. 7 (1949) in *Respectfully Quoted: A Dictionary of Quotations* (1989), Bartleby.com, https://www.bartleby.com/73/465.html.

Chapter 14: Protect Your Head in Battle: The Helmet of Salvation

1. Adhikari, "Top 10 Ancient Roman Armor and Costume."

2. Encyclopaedia Britannica Editors, "Helmet," *Encyclopædia Britannica*, July 20, 2017, https://www.britannica.com/technology/helmet-armour.

3. Staci Michaels (artist) and Tom Hopkins (artist), "Guard Your Mind," *Be a Champion*, N-Crease Music, 1997, CD.

Chapter 15: Queen, Grab Your Sword: The Sword of the Spirit

1. Adhikari, "Top 10 Ancient Roman Armor and Costume"; Encyclopaedia Britannica Editors, "Legion," *Encyclopædia Britannica*, May 05, 2009, https:// www.britannica.com/topic/legion.

2. C. H. Spurgeon, "The Sword of the Spirit," sermon delivered on April 19, 1891, *The Complete Works of C. H. Spurgeon, Volume 37* (Delmarva Publications, Inc., 2015), no. 2201.

Part Four: Awakening to Your Divine Purpose

1. *Merriam-Webster.com Dictionary*, s.v. "awake," https://www.merriam-web ster.com/dictionary/awake.

Chapter 17: An Unlikely Hero

1. See Acts 13:9.
2. David Halberstam, *The Best and the Brightest*, 1st ed. (New York: Random House, 1972).
3. See Hebrews 11:7.
4. See Hebrews 11:17; see also vv. 8–20.
5. See Luke 1.
6. Luke 22:42.

Chapter 19: Don't Retreat—Reload!

1. David & Nicole Binion, featuring Steffany Gretzinger, David Binion and Mitch Wong, songwriters, "Living Proof," *Glory of Eden (Live)* (Brentwood, TN: Integrity Music, 2020).

Staci Wallace is an author, entrepreneur, business consultant, personal coach and leading voice in women's empowerment. She is the founder of EMwomen, an organization that has helped women across the world overcome abuse and exploitation, focusing on raising up and training leaders to change their world with the truth of God's Word. As a sought-after keynote speaker, she has shared the stage with five U.S. presidents, world leaders, athletes, motivational speakers and leaders of various industries. Currently, Staci serves as executive vice president of strategy for a global telecom company, giving her an even greater voice in the marketplace and global business development landscape. Staci and her husband, Larry, and their two children make their home in the Dallas/Fort Worth area of Texas.

You can learn more about Staci at StaciWallace.com and more about her passion for empowering women at EMwomen.com. Staci loves connecting with her readers and hearing their stories. You can connect with her through her social media accounts at:

Facebook: www.facebook.com/staciwallace
Twitter: @StaciWallace
Instagram: @StaciWallace